DINNER'S IN THE OVEN

DINNER'S IN THE OVEN

SIMPLE ONE-PAN MEALS

RUKMINI IYER

Photographs by David Loftus

CONTENTS

INTRODUCTION

This is not a conventional cookbook in that once you've tried a few recipes and are happy with the principle (stick everything in a roasting pan, pop the pan in the oven, and serve), you can, and indeed should, use the infographics and charts in the chapter openers, transferring useful information like oven temperatures and cooking times, to create any number of your own recipes. In the mood for salmon with roasted red peppers, onions, and thyme rather than chicken? Swap them, and borrow the oven temperature and timings as needed. Got vine tomatoes staring at you reproachfully from the fruit bowl? Stick them in and let them get gloriously blistered with everything else.

Use roasting pans, baking dishes (glass, ceramic), or shallow casserole pans—anything ovenproof will do. And for recipes that feed a crowd, like the smoky roast sausages and sweet potatoes (page 94), consider using the metal broiler pan that comes standard with most ovens.

The recipes in each chapter are organized by speed—toward the beginning of each you'll find recipes that roast in under 30 minutes, progressing to dishes that you can leave in the oven for an hour or so. A few, designed for lazy weekend lunches, will sit happily for three hours after minimal prep, like the harissa lamb (page 102) or Filipino slow-roast pork (page 101).

Many recipes will serve four, and any leftovers make for really superior next-day lunches. The orzo with broccoli (page 130), avocado and chicken salad with rice (page 116), or spelt with chorizo (page 162) are particularly good if you plan to induce lunchbox envy among your colleagues.

While the design of the recipes is to cook everything in the same pan, which, in the grains chapter, works particularly well with pearled barley, spelt, and couscous, if it is significantly quicker to put a pot of boiling water on for accompanying carbs (rice or pasta), then I have suggested that instead. The timings in the recipes are such that your oven-cooked main dish and low-effort side will be finished at the same time—always preferable.

The nicest thing about oven-made meals is that they are both versatile and forgiving. They require the barest minimum in terms of effort—a little light chopping to start, then tasting and adjusting the salt or lemon juice at the end. Most importantly they leave you free to do something else while dinner looks after itself—have a bath, help the children with their homework, or, my preferred option, flop on the sofa with a glass of wine, reading Nora Ephron on crisp potatoes and true love. (Ideally with crisp potatoes roasting in the oven.)

THE PANTRY

A well-stocked pantry allows you to transform staple fresh ingredients—chicken, fish, vegetables—into something different and interesting each time you put dinner in the oven. Have the following on hand:

QUICK-FIX FLAVOR ESSENTIALS

SHARP: Keep jars of Dijon mustard, olive tapenade, pesto, and harissa on standby in the fridge to dress even the simplest dish.

SWEET: Root vegetables, chicken, and sausages all benefit from the judicious use of sweetness, alongside other flavors. Try honey, maple syrup, or agave—they all combine well with mustard and spices.

SAVORY: You don't have to get fussy with the type of salt that you use—this book calls for flaked sea salt, but by all means use finely ground if you prefer.

CRUNCH

Texture is all-important for an oven-cooked meal, as it is for any dish—keep almonds, hazelnuts, pistachios, and pine nuts in the fridge and panko breadcrumbs in the pantry to use as a quick topping for fish or vegetable dishes.

SPICES

These add instant interest and can be combined in endless variations. Keep the classics—ground cumin, coriander, fennel seeds, and smoked paprika—alongside the now popular and readily available sumac, ras el hanout, and za'atar.

OIL

Olive oil, the key to successful roasting, will do for almost anything. Try toasted sesame for Asian dishes, or coconut oil if you are that way inclined. Lots of people aren't—it's fine.

FRESH

You are always going to need onions and garlic, so keep them in the pantry, and have ginger in the fridge. Lemons and limes are essential standbys for sharpness and interest, either as zest or juice—you'll often find a squeeze of lemon juice a more effective seasoning than an extra pinch of salt.

FISH

QUICK, FRESH, AND NUTRITIOUS, OVEN-
COOKED FISH WORKS WITH A VARIETY OF
FLAVORS, VEGETABLES, AND TOPPINGS.

1 FISH

CHOOSE YOUR FISH

TUNA

SALMON FILLET

MACKEREL

SHRIMP

SARDINE

TROUT

COD/POLLACK

LEMON SOLE

SEE PAGE 23 AFOR ROASTING TIMES

ADD FLAVORINGS

LEMON

LIME

GINGER

GARLIC

PESTO

CHILE

TAPENADE

HARISSA

TEXTURE

PANKO BREADCRUMBS

ALMONDS

PINE NUTS

ADD VEGETABLES

FENNEL

TOMATO

SHALLOT

LEEK

RED ONION

RED BELL PEPPER

ZUCCHINI

ASPARAGUS

MUSHROOM

ADD SEASONINGS + HERBS

THYME

DILL

BASIL

MINT

CILANTRO

PARSLEY

OLIVE OIL

SEA SALT

ROASTING TIMES FOR FISH

FISH	OVEN TEMPERATURE	SUGGESTED TIME
SHRIMP (large or extra-large)	BROILER	5 MINUTES
COD/POLLACK (approx. 4 ounces [115g] fillet)	400°F [200°C]	15 MINUTES
SALMON (approx. 4 ounces [115g] fillet)	400°F [200°C]	20 TO 25 MINUTES
TROUT (14 ounces [400g] whole, cleaned)	400°F [200°C]	20 MINUTES
TROUT (approx. 3½ ounces [100g] fillet)	400°F [200°C]	10 MINUTES
MACKEREL (approx. 3 ounces [85g] fillet)	400°F [200°C]	10 TO 15 MINUTES
SARDINES (whole, cleaned)	400°F [200°C]	10 MINUTES
SEA BASS (approx. 3 ounces [85g] fillet)	400°F [200°C]	8 MINUTES
LEMON SOLE (approx. 3½ ounces [100g] fillet)	400°F [200°C]	10 MINUTES
TUNA (approx. 4 ounces [115g] fillet, 1 to 1½ inches [2.5 to 4cm] thick)	425°F [220°C]	5 MINUTES medium-rare 8 MINUTES well done

Note: The thinner your fillet, the quicker it will cook, no matter the weight. A cod fillet cut from the tail, which is thinner, will cook faster than one cut from the middle, which is thicker, even though they might both weigh 4 ounces [115g], so bear this in mind when using the chart.

And, of course, no two ovens heat alike, so be prepared to leave the fish in an extra couple of minutes if needed.

LIME & GINGER BROILED SHRIMP WITH MUSHROOMS & CILANTRO

Under a scorchingly hot broiler, shrimp are so quick and easy to cook. This makes a lovely starter, or a more substantial meal served with a bowl of fluffy white rice.

Serves: 2
Prep: 7 minutes
Cook: 5 minutes

½ pound [230g] large shrimp
½ pound [230g] mixed shiitake
  and oyster mushrooms
1 lime, zest and juice, plus
  wedges to serve
1 inch [2.5cm] ginger, grated
2 cloves garlic, grated
1 tablespoon olive oil
½ fresh red chile, thinly sliced
3 scallions, thinly sliced
Sea salt or fish sauce
A handful of fresh cilantro,
  roughly chopped

1. Preheat your broiler to its highest setting with a rack in the uppermost position.

2. In a shallow roasting pan or rimmed baking sheet, combine the shrimp, mushrooms, lime zest and juice, ginger, garlic, olive oil, chile, and scallions. Season with sea salt or fish sauce and arrange in an even layer.

3. Place under the broiler for 5 minutes, until the shrimp are evenly pink and cooked through. Taste and season with more sea salt or fish sauce as required. Scatter over the chopped cilantro and serve immediately with lime wedges.

OLIVE & PINE NUT–CRUSTED COD WITH ROASTED RED ONION & CHERRY TOMATOES

White fish stands up so well to strong flavors—and the textural contrast with the pine nut crust makes this a very pleasing dinner overall. By all means, substitute the cod with pollack or your preferred sustainably caught white fish.

Serves: 2
Prep: 10 minutes
Cook: 15 minutes

2 cod fillets or steaks (approx. 12 ounces [340g] total)
12 ounces [340g] cherry tomatoes on the vine
1 red onion, thinly sliced
4 teaspoons olive tapenade
4 teaspoons [15g] pine nuts
4 teaspoons [15g] panko breadcrumbs
Sea salt
Olive oil
Freshly ground black pepper

Note: Use fresh white breadcrumbs instead of panko breadcrumbs if more readily available.

1. Preheat your oven to 400°F [200°C] with a rack positioned in the upper third. Arrange the cod fillets, cherry tomatoes, and onion in a roasting pan or baking dish. Spread the tapenade evenly on the cod fillets.

2. Lightly crush the pine nuts in a mortar and pestle, then mix them with the panko breadcrumbs, a pinch of sea salt, and a tablespoon of olive oil. Pat this mixture on top of the tapenade.

3. Drizzle a little olive oil over the cherry tomatoes and onion and season with sea salt and freshly ground black pepper. Pop the pan into the oven and roast for 15 minutes, until the topping is crisp and the cod is cooked through. Serve immediately.

HERB-STUFFED TROUT WITH ROASTED SWEET POTATOES & RED ONION

Whole trout are so easy to cook—here, a very simple herb and lemon stuffing lets the flavor of the fish take center stage. Be sure to season the fish well with sea salt inside and out before roasting.

Serves: 2
Prep: 15 minutes
Cook: 40 minutes

1½ pounds [680g] sweet potatoes, peeled and very thinly sliced
1 red onion, thinly sliced
2 tablespoons olive oil
Sea salt and freshly ground black pepper
½ small bunch fresh tarragon or rosemary, leaves only
½ small bunch fresh oregano, leaves only
2 small trout (approx. 14 ounces [400g] each), cleaned
4 cloves garlic, roughly chopped
½ small lemon, thinly sliced

1. Preheat the oven to 400°F [200°C]. Mix the sweet potato slices, red onion, olive oil, 1 teaspoon sea salt, and a good grind of black pepper in a roasting pan or large baking dish, along with half the herbs, then pop into the oven and roast for 20 minutes.

2. Meanwhile, season the cavity of the trout with sea salt and freshly ground black pepper, then stuff with the remaining herbs, the garlic, and the lemon slices.

3. Once the sweet potatoes have had 20 minutes, top with the stuffed trout and scatter over 2 teaspoons sea salt. Return to the oven and roast a further 20 minutes, until the trout is just cooked through (it will just begin to flake when prodded with a fork). Serve immediately.

STEAM-ROASTED SALMON & BROCCOLI WITH LIME, GINGER, GARLIC & CHILE

I could eat this punchy dressing—packed with fish sauce, peanuts, lime, and cilantro—slathered over almost anything. It works particularly well to cut through the rich salmon, and the peanuts provide wonderful texture. While the salmon and broccoli cook, you can focus on the light chopping and stirring to put the dressing together. If cooking for children, leave out the chile and add it to your portion.

Serves: 4
Prep: 10 minutes
Cook: 20 to 25 minutes

1 small head broccoli, cut into small florets
2 cloves garlic, grated
2 tablespoons sesame or vegetable oil
4 salmon fillets (approx. 1¾ pounds [800g] total)
2 scallions, thinly sliced
1 inch [2.5cm] ginger, grated
1 fresh red chile, thinly sliced
2 tablespoons fish sauce
¼ cup [60ml] vegetable oil
Zest and juice of 2 limes
½ cup [30g] finely chopped fresh cilantro
6 tablespoons [55g] roughly chopped peanuts

1. Preheat the oven to 400°F [200°C]. Place the broccoli in a roasting pan or large baking dish, scatter over the grated garlic, drizzle with the sesame oil, and toss well to mix.

2. Place the salmon fillets in the roasting pan, cover the pan tightly with foil, then transfer to the oven and bake for 20 to 25 minutes, until the salmon is cooked through to your liking.

3. Meanwhile, mix together the scallions, ginger, chile, fish sauce, vegetable oil, lime zest and juice, cilantro, and peanuts. Taste and adjust the fish sauce and lime juice as you wish.

4. Remove the roasting pan from the oven and generously coat the salmon with some of the dressing. Drizzle the remaining dressing over the broccoli and serve immediately.

MACKEREL & RHUBARB

This light, refreshing, Scandinavian-inspired dish makes a lovely starter for a dinner party. The rhubarb, a perfect foil to the mackerel, is roasted for just long enough to cook through but still hold its shape.

Serves: 4
Prep: 15 minutes
Cook: 15 minutes

1½ pounds [680g] rhubarb, cut into even lengths
5 shallots, very thinly sliced
2½ tablespoons white wine vinegar
1 tablespoon olive oil
1 tablespoon sugar
6 mackerel fillets, pinbones removed (you can ask your fishmonger to do this)
¼ cup [30g] skinned hazelnuts
½ cucumber, shaved into ribbons
1 teaspoon sea salt
¼ cup [10g] roughly chopped fresh dill
6 tablespoons [85g] crème fraîche

1. Preheat your oven to 400°F [200°C]. Place the rhubarb, shallots, 1½ table-spoons of the vinegar, the olive oil, and the sugar in a roasting pan or large baking dish and mix well.

2. Lay the mackerel fillets on top of the rhubarb, cover the dish with foil, then transfer to the oven and bake for 10 minutes.

3. After 10 minutes, remove the foil and scatter over the hazelnuts. Return the pan to the oven and continue to bake, uncovered, for a further 5 minutes.

4. Meanwhile, mix the cucumber, sea salt, the remaining 1 tablespoon vinegar, and half of the dill.

5. Serve the mackerel and rhubarb with the cucumber salad and crème fraîche and sprinkle with the remaining dill.

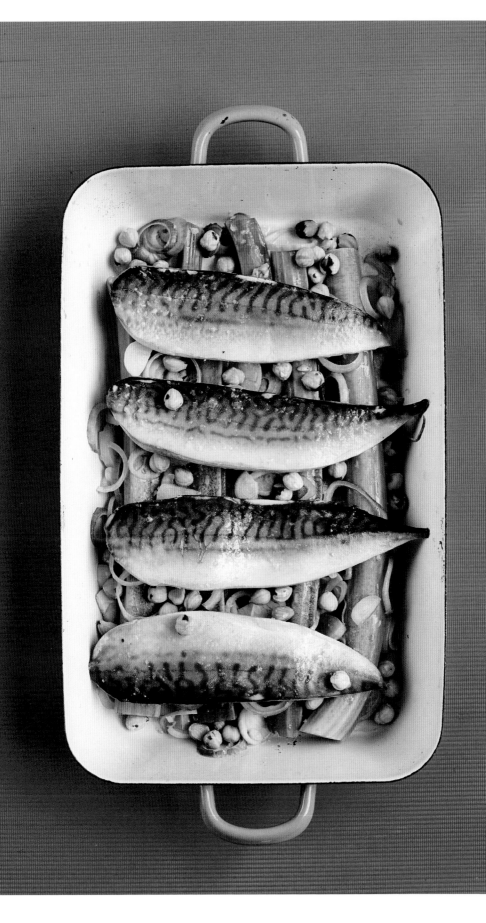

SARDINES WITH PAPRIKA-ROASTED PEPPERS, TOMATOES, CHILES & ALMONDS

I could eat these silky paprika-roasted peppers and tomatoes with their crunchy almond topping just by themselves, but add the sardines and you have a lovely, complete little dish. The fishmonger will be able to clean the sardines for you, for added speed at home.

Serves: 2
Prep: 10 minutes
Cook: 25 minutes

2 red bell peppers, seeded and thinly sliced
½ pound [230g] cherry tomatoes on the vine
1 red chile, half thinly sliced, the other half finely chopped
2 teaspoons paprika
3 tablespoons olive oil
Zest of 1 lemon
½ cup [50g] sliced almonds, roughly broken up
1 teaspoon sea salt
6 sardines, cleaned and rinsed
A handful of torn fresh basil leaves
Lemon wedges, to serve

1. Preheat the oven to 400°F [200°C]. Combine the red bell peppers, cherry tomatoes, the sliced red chile, the paprika, and 2 tablespoons of the olive oil in a roasting pan or large baking dish, and mix well. Transfer to the oven and roast for 15 minutes.

2. Meanwhile, mix together the lemon zest, the chopped red chile, the sliced almonds, sea salt, and the remaining 1 tablespoon olive oil. Stuff as much of it into the sardines as will fit.

3. Once the vegetables have had 15 minutes in the oven, lay the sardines on top and scatter the rest of the almond mixture over the vegetables. Return to the oven for a further 10 minutes.

4. Sprinkle with the basil and serve hot, with lemon wedges alongside.

CHICKEN

THE CLASSIC ROASTED DINNER: INFINITELY VERSATILE AND PARTICULARLY GOOD WITH EARTHY ROOT VEGETABLES, STRONG HERBS, AND SPICES.

2 CHICKEN

CHOOSE YOUR CHICKEN

DRUMSTICK

THIGH

BREAST

WING

SEE PAGE 43 FOR ROASTING TIMES

ADD VEGETABLES

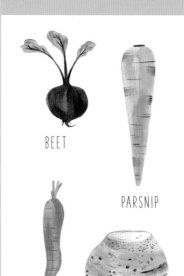

BEET

PARSNIP

CARROT   CELERY ROOT

FENNEL

BUTTERNUT SQUASH

POTATO

SWEET POTATO

ADD AROMATICS

SCALLION

LEEK

GARLIC

RED ONION

YELLOW ONION

ADD FLAVORINGS

SPICY

CORIANDER SEED   FENNEL SEED   SMOKED PAPRIKA

CUMIN   SUMAC

CHILE

HARISSA   RAS EL HANOUT

SHARP

MUSTARD   LEMON   LIME   GINGER

SWEET

HONEY   MAPLE   AGAVE

ADD SALT & OIL

SEA SALT

OLIVE OIL

COCONUT OIL

SESAME OIL

SUNFLOWER OIL

ADD HERBS

SAGE   BASIL

CILANTRO   ROSEMARY

PARSLEY

LEMONGRASS

KAFFIR LIME

OREGANO

THYME

DILL   MINT

ROASTING TIMES FOR CHICKEN

CHICKEN	OVEN TEMPERATURE	SUGGESTED TIME
CHICKEN WINGS (all in one layer)	325°F [170°C]	**40 MINUTES** increase to 400°F [200°C], then another **20 MINUTES**
BONELESS CHICKEN BREAST HALVES (approx. 6 ounces [170g])	400°F [200°C]	**25 MINUTES**
BONE-IN CHICKEN THIGHS & DRUMSTICKS	400°F [200°C]	**45 MINUTES**
WHOLE CHICKEN (5 pounds [2.3kg])	350°F [180°C]	**1 HOUR 30 MINUTES** increase to 400°F [200°C], then another **30 MINUTES**

Note: Adjust the time for your chicken depending on weight—smaller chicken breasts (e.g., 4 ounces [115g]) will take only 20 minutes, while 7 ounces [200g] will take up to 30 minutes.

All chicken will benefit from resting for at least 5 minutes before serving.

ROASTED CHICKEN WITH FENNEL, LEMON, SHALLOTS, GARLIC & MUSTARD MAYO

This is as good for a quick weeknight meal as it is for easy entertaining, and an excellent way to use up any impulse-bought fennel that might be languishing at the back of the fridge. If you can find skin-on chicken breasts, you'll get lovely crispy chicken skin as a bonus, but this works just as well otherwise. A quick pantry sauce made from mustard and mayonnaise brings the dish together.

Serves: 4
Prep: 10 minutes
Cook: 30 minutes

1 large bulb fennel, thinly sliced
12 shallots, quartered
1 lemon, cut into eighths
6 cloves garlic, smashed
A few sprigs of fresh thyme
4 boneless skin-on chicken
   breasts
Sea salt and freshly ground
   black pepper
Olive oil

MUSTARD MAYO

4 heaping tablespoons
   mayonnaise
2 heaping tablespoons Dijon
   mustard
2 teaspoons honey

1. Preheat the oven to 400°F [200°C].

2. Place the fennel, shallots, lemon wedges, garlic, and thyme in a roasting pan or large baking dish, and put the chicken breasts on top. Season generously with sea salt and freshly ground black pepper and drizzle everything generously with olive oil.

3. Mix well to make sure the vegetables and chicken are evenly coated in the oil, then transfer to the oven and roast for 30 minutes, until the chicken is cooked through.

4. For the mustard mayo, mix together the mayonnaise, mustard, and honey and set aside. Let rest for 5 minutes out of the oven, then serve with the sauce.

SIMPLE ROASTED CHICKEN & BELL PEPPERS

Very simple and super-quick, this classic dish makes for an easy weeknight dinner. Serve with some good baguette or similar on the side to mop up the peppers. My friend Laura, a good cook from a family of culinary excellence, suggests adding some sliced Spanish chorizo to the pan, which works beautifully.

Serves: 4
Prep: 10 minutes
Cook: 35 minutes

4 large boneless skin-on
   chicken breasts
2 red bell peppers, seeded and
   cut into ½-inch [1.5cm] slices
2 yellow peppers, seeded and
   cut into ½-inch [1.5cm] slices
2 red onions, cut into eighths
6 cloves garlic, smashed
6 sprigs of fresh thyme or
   rosemary
Sea salt and freshly ground
   black pepper
Olive oil

Note: If you prefer, you can use thighs and drumsticks; cook them for 1 hour and 30 minutes.

To add a smoky Spanish note, add 1 tablespoon smoked paprika to the dish before roasting; or alternatively, for a citrusy finish, add 1 tablespoon sumac.

1. Preheat your oven to 400°F [200°C].

2. Place the chicken, bell peppers, onions, garlic, and herbs in one very large roasting pan. Sprinkle evenly with a good pinch of sea salt and freshly ground black pepper. Drizzle generously with olive oil and give everything a really good mix with your hands.

3. Place the pan in the oven and roast for 35 minutes, until the chicken is golden brown and cooked through and the peppers are lovely and caramelized. Allow to rest for 5 minutes, then serve hot.

ROASTED CHICKEN, SQUASH & RED ONION WITH LEMON & ROSEMARY

Throwing lemon wedges into a roasting pan to caramelize is my best friend Emma's technique, learned from a very battered copy of *BBC Good Food* magazine. Serve this flavor-packed dish with a well-dressed arugula or spinach salad on the side.

Serves: 2
Prep: 10 minutes
Cook: 1 hour

1 pound [455g] bone-in, skin-on chicken thighs and drumsticks
¾ pound [340g] squash of your choice, cut into wedges
1 red onion, cut into eighths
1 lemon, cut into eighths
6 cloves garlic, smashed
4 or 5 sprigs of fresh rosemary
Olive oil
2 to 3 tablespoons honey
Sea salt and freshly ground black pepper

Note: You can use summer squash or winter squash in this dish. Winter squash will need to be seeded and, if you like, peeled before cooking.

If time permits, the chicken will taste even better if you cook it slowly at 325°F [170°C] for 1 hour, turn the heat up to 400°F [200°C], and cook for a further 30 minutes to crisp the skin.

1. Preheat your oven to 400°F [200°C].

2. Place the chicken thighs and drumsticks, squash, red onion, lemon, garlic, and rosemary in a roasting pan or large baking dish. Splash on a generous amount of olive oil, drizzle on the honey, then season generously with sea salt and freshly ground black pepper. Mix together with your hands so that everything is evenly coated.

3. Place the pan in the oven to roast for 1 hour, until the chicken skin is crispy and golden. Let rest for 5 minutes, then serve hot.

SPICY CHIPOTLE CHICKEN WINGS WITH SWEET POTATO WEDGES, CILANTRO & LIME YOGURT

For a summery outdoor lunch or game-night snack, you'd be hard-pressed to find a better option than these sticky, spicy chicken wings. Serve with a glass of something chilled.

Serves: 4
Prep: 10 minutes
Cook: 1 hour

1¾ pounds [800g] chicken wings, separated into wingettes and drumettes
1¾ pounds [800g] sweet potatoes, peeled and cut into 1-inch [2.5cm] wedges
2 teaspoons chipotle chile powder
1 teaspoon smoked paprika
1 tablespoon dark brown sugar
3 tablespoons olive oil
Sea salt
Zest and juice of 1 lime, plus lime wedges, to serve
4 to 5 tablespoons Greek yogurt
A handful of fresh cilantro leaves, chopped, plus more to serve

1. Preheat the oven to 325°F [170°C]. Place the chicken wings and sweet potato wedges in a large roasting pan or rimmed baking sheet.

2. Mix together the chipotle chile powder, smoked paprika, brown sugar, olive oil, 2 teaspoons sea salt, and half of the lime zest and juice. Pour the mixture over the chicken and sweet potatoes and mix well with your hands to coat evenly. Transfer to the oven and roast for 40 minutes.

3. Turn the heat up to 400°F [200°C] and roast for a further 20 minutes, to crisp the chicken skin.

4. Meanwhile, mix together the yogurt, chopped cilantro, remaining lime zest and juice, and a pinch of sea salt. Set aside.

5. Sprinkle the chicken wings and sweet potatoes with cilantro leaves and serve with lime wedges and the yogurt dip alongside.

OVEN-ROASTED
COQ AU VIN

I first made this dish after rifling through my fridge and finding the harmonious combination of pancetta, chicken thighs, and mushrooms. Add in a few leaves from a bay tree and my laziness in not wanting to have to stir anything, and this crispy, delicious version of coq au vin was born, to general approval an hour and a half later.

Serves: 4
Prep: 10 minutes
Cook: 1 hour 30 minutes

4 bone-in, skin-on chicken leg
    quarters (about 3 pounds
    [1.4kg] total)
6 ounces [170g] pancetta,
    cubed
½ pound [230g] large cremini
    mushrooms
5 cloves garlic, smashed
½ pound [230g] shallots,
    halved
3 bay leaves, preferably fresh
2 or 3 sprigs of fresh rosemary
2 tablespoons butter, softened
Sea salt and freshly ground
    black pepper
1 cup [240ml] red wine

1. Preheat your oven to 350°F [180°C]. Place the chicken, pancetta, mushrooms, garlic, shallots, bay leaves, and rosemary in a large roasting pan and smear everything with the butter. Season with sea salt and freshly ground black pepper, then transfer to the oven and roast for 40 minutes.

2. Turn the heat up to 400°F [200°C] and cook for a further 40 minutes, until the chicken is cooked through and a lovely deep golden brown. Splash the wine into the pan around the chicken and return to the oven for a further 10 minutes. Allow to rest for a few minutes before serving.

CHICKEN WITH CHORIZO, CHICKPEAS & TOMATOES

This substantial stew gives you all the depth of flavor of a slow-cooked pot roast, but with the textural advantage of wonderfully crispy, golden chicken. All you need for this dish is some really good bread to mop up the sauce. Anna and Daniel, who taste-tested this dish for me, suggest a nice glass of mazanilla sherry on the side.

Serves: 4
Prep: 10 minutes
Cook: 1 hour 30 minutes

1 yellow onion, finely chopped
2 cloves garlic, chopped
2 sprigs of fresh rosemary
¼ pound [115g] Spanish chorizo, roughly chopped
One 14½-ounce [400g] can chickpeas, rinsed and drained
One 14½-ounce [400g] can tomatoes
1¼ cups [300ml] water
Sea salt and freshly ground black pepper
4 bone-in, skin-on chicken leg quarters (about 3 pounds [1.4kg] total)
1 tablespoon olive oil

1. Preheat the oven to 350°F [180°C]. Place the onion, garlic, rosemary, chorizo, chickpeas, and tomatoes in a large roasting pan, and use the water to rinse out the tomato can before pouring it into the pan. Season well with sea salt and freshly ground black pepper.

2. Arrange the chicken legs on the tomato mixture and drizzle with the olive oil. Sprinkle with sea salt and black pepper, then transfer to the oven and roast for 40 minutes.

3. Turn the heat up to 400°F [200°C] and roast for a further 50 minutes, until the chicken is golden brown and cooked through. Taste the sauce, season as needed with sea salt and black pepper. Allow to rest for a few minutes, then serve hot.

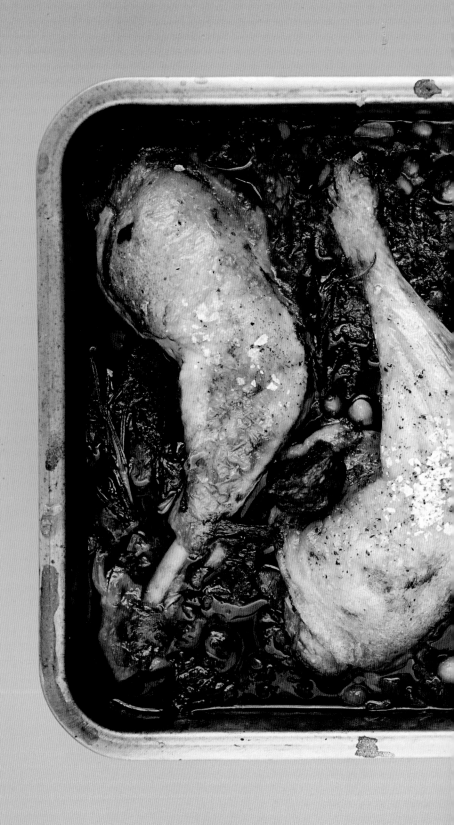

VEGETABLES

FROM QUICK SIDES TO HEARTY, FILLING
MAIN MEALS—COMBINE SEVERAL FOR A
VEGETARIAN POTLUCK OR PICK ONE FOR
A WEEKNIGHT DINNER.

3 VEGETABLES

CHOOSE YOUR WINTER VEGETABLE

CAULIFLOWER

CELERY ROOT

BUTTERNUT SQUASH

PARSNIP

BROCCOLI

BRUSSELS SPROUTS

SWEET POTATO

SEE PAGE 61 FOR ROASTING TIMES

OR

OR SUMMER VEGETABLE

CORN

ASPARAGUS

TOMATO

BROCCOLINI

EGGPLANT

ZUCCHINI

RED BELL PEPPER

MUSHROOM

OKRA

SEE PAGE 61 FOR ROASTING TIMES

+

ADD AROMATICS

SCALLION

LEEK

GARLIC

RED ONION

YELLOW ONION

ADD SEASONINGS & FLAVORINGS

SEA SALT

OLIVE OIL

CORIANDER SEED

GINGER

CUMIN

SMOKED PAPRIKA

CHILE

SUMAC

LEMON

LIME

RAS EL HANOUT

CRUNCH

ALMONDS

HAZELNUTS

CASHEWS

PINE NUTS

+

ADD DAIRY

YOGURT

MOZZARELLA

HALLOUMI

GOAT CHEESE

FETA

+

ADD GREENS & HERBS

ARUGULA

SPINACH

WATERCRESS

HERBS

BASIL

CILANTRO

PARSLEY

SAGE

MINT

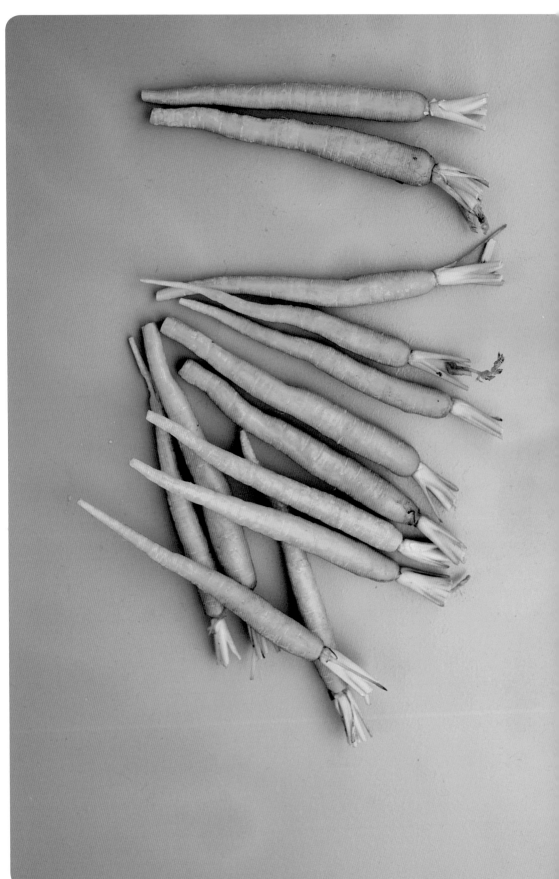

ROASTING TIMES FOR VEGETABLES

VEGETABLE	OVEN TEMPERATURE	SUGGESTED TIME
CAULIFLOWER (smallish florets)	400°F [200°C]	40 TO 45 MINUTES
CELERY ROOT (¾-in [2cm] chunks)	400°F [200°C]	45 MINUTES
BUTTERNUT SQUASH (½-inch [1.5cm] chunks)	400°F [200°C]	1 HOUR
BROCCOLI (smallish florets)	400°F [200°C] (uncovered pan) (covered pan)	40 TO 45 MINUTES 20 TO 25 MINUTES
BROCCOLINI	400°F [200°C]	30 MINUTES
SWEET POTATO (¾-in [2cm] chunks)	400°F [200°C]	40 TO 45 MINUTES
BRUSSELS SPROUTS (halved)	400°F [200°C]	25 TO 30 MINUTES
CORN	400°F [200°C]	30 MINUTES
ASPARAGUS	400°F [200°C]	10 TO 13 MINUTES
TOMATOES (quartered large or whole cherry tomatoes)	400°F [200°C]	15 MINUTES
ZUCCHINI (½-inch [1.5cm] slices)	400°F [200°C]	40 MINUTES
EGGPLANT (cut into eighths)	400°F [200°C]	30 TO 40 MINUTES
RED BELL PEPPERS (sliced)	400°F [200°C]	30 TO 40 MINUTES
OKRA	400°F [200°C]	30 TO 40 MINUTES
MUSHROOMS	400°F [200°C]	20 TO 25 MINUTES

PAPRIKA-ROASTED CORN WITH SCALLIONS, FETA & LIME

Once you've tried cooking corn like this, you'll be hard-pressed to go back to simmering it on the stove. The smoky paprika, feta, and lime work beautifully with the roasted corn, with added crunch and freshness from the scallions. Serve as part of a vegetarian buffet table or alongside fish dishes.

Serves: 5
Prep: 5 minutes
Cook: 30 minutes

5 ears corn, shucked
Olive oil
2 teaspoons paprika
A large pinch of sea salt
1 lime, halved
5 scallions, thinly sliced
⅔ cup [75g] crumbled feta

1. Preheat your oven to 400°F [200°C] with a rack positioned in the upper third.

2. Place the corn in a roasting pan or large baking dish and drizzle with a generous amount of olive oil. Sprinkle with the paprika and sea salt and rub the seasonings into the corn. Transfer to the oven and roast for 30 minutes.

3. Remove the pan from the oven. Squeeze the juice from the lime halves over the corn, scatter over the scallions and feta, and serve hot.

BEET, DILL & GORGONZOLA TARTS WITH CAPERS & WALNUTS

These grown-up tarts need only a lightly dressed arugula salad on the side for a quick, filling, and interesting weekend lunch. Baking the tarts at a slightly higher temperature ensures a nice crisp base and eliminates the need for an egg wash. They're best served hot, but leftovers make a very acceptable picnic lunch.

Serves: 6
Prep: 15 minutes
Cook: 30 minutes

½ pound [230g] small raw
   beets, peeled and thinly sliced
1 tablespoon olive oil
1 teaspoon red wine vinegar
Sea salt
One 10-by-15-inch [25-by-
   38cm] sheet frozen puff
   pastry, thawed
⅔ cup [75g] crumbled
   Gorgonzola cheese
2 tablespoons capers
¼ cup [10g] chopped fresh dill
½ cup [50g] roughly chopped
   walnuts

1. Preheat the oven to 425°F [220°C]. Mix the beet slices with the olive oil, red wine vinegar, and 1 teaspoon sea salt, and set aside.

2. Cut the puff pastry sheet into six squares and place on a parchment paper–lined rimmed baking sheet. Lay beet slices in overlapping layers on each square, leaving a ½-inch [1.5cm] border, then scatter over the Gorgonzola, capers, and half of the dill.

3. Transfer to the oven and bake for 25 minutes, then scatter over the chopped walnuts and return to the oven for a further 5 minutes.

4. Sprinkle with the rest of the dill and a tiny pinch of sea salt before serving.

FRENCH TOMATO & MUSTARD TART WITH TARRAGON

This recipe originates with Mme. Renaud, the mother of my French exchange student, Sophie. At thirteen, I watched with both interest and apprehension (having some doubts about both mustard and tomatoes) as Mme. Renaud made the tart, and was absolutely transported on first bite. It tastes like summer and holidays.

Serves: 4
Prep: 10 minutes
Cook: 30 minutes

One 10-by-15-inch [25-by-38cm] sheet frozen puff pastry, thawed
2½ tablespoons Dijon mustard
¾ pound [340g] vine-ripened tomatoes, thinly sliced
4 teaspoons [5g] finely chopped fresh tarragon
1 teaspoon sea salt
Freshly ground black pepper
1 tablespoon extra-virgin olive oil

1. Preheat the oven to 425°F [220°C]. Place the puff pastry on a parchment paper–lined rimmed baking sheet. Spread the mustard all over, leaving a ¾-inch [2cm] border around the edges. Arrange the sliced tomatoes on the mustard. Sprinkle on the tarragon, sea salt, and freshly ground black pepper and drizzle with the olive oil.

2. Transfer to the oven and bake for 25 to 30 minutes, until the edges of the tart are golden brown and crisp. Serve immediately.

ROASTED EGGPLANTS WITH MOZZARELLA, CHILE, LEMON & PARSLEY

In this recipe, the roasted eggplants are marinated post-cooking in a dressing packed with lemon and chile. A generous topping of marinated mozzarella adds both flavor and texture, making this the perfect addition to a vegetarian buffet.

Serves: 4
Prep: 10 to 15 minutes
Cook: 40 minutes

2 large eggplants
Sea salt
3 to 4 tablespoons olive oil
6 tablespoons extra-virgin olive oil
Zest and juice of 2 lemons
1 bunch fresh flat-leaf parsley, leaves chopped
1 fresh red chile, seeded and finely chopped
½ pound [230g] buffalo mozzarella, roughly torn into chunks

Note: Take the mozzarella out of the fridge 30 minutes before using and drain in a sieve.

1. Preheat the oven to 400°F [200°C]. Cut the tops off the eggplants and slice them lengthwise in half, then cut each half lengthwise into quarters. Place the slices in a roasting pan or large baking dish, add a generous sprinkle of sea salt, and drizzle with the olive oil. Mix well with your hands to evenly coat the eggplant slices, then arrange them in a single layer. Pop the pan into the oven and roast for 40 minutes.

2. Meanwhile, whisk together the extra-virgin olive oil, lemon zest and juice, parsley, and chile. Season to taste with sea salt, then drizzle a few tablespoons of the dressing over the torn mozzarella and set aside.

3. As soon as the eggplants are ready, drizzle the remaining dressing over them and turn them gently until thoroughly coated. Allow them to sit in the dressing for 5 minutes, then add the marinated mozzarella and serve warm.

SPICED ROASTED CAULIFLOWER, SWEET POTATO & OKRA WITH YOGURT & ALMONDS

This smoky, roasted vegetable dish gives you all the flavor of a slow-cooked curry, without any of the stirring. If you feel like extra carbs alongside, serve it with a bowl of brown rice or bulgur wheat.

Serves: 4
Prep: 10 minutes
Cook: 40 minutes

1 extra-large cauliflower or
   2 small cauliflowers, cut
   into small florets
2 medium sweet potatoes,
   peeled and cut into ¾-inch
   [2cm] chunks
6 cloves garlic, minced
2 inches [5cm] ginger, minced
4 teaspoons paprika
4 teaspoons ground cumin
½ cup [120ml] olive oil
Sea salt
¾ pound [340g] okra, left whole
¾ cup [180g] yogurt
Juice of 1 lemon
¾ cup [80g] sliced almonds,
   toasted
½ red onion, thinly sliced
A handful of torn fresh mint or
   cilantro leaves

1. Preheat your oven to 400°F [200°C].

2. Place the cauliflower florets and sweet potato chunks in a large roasting pan. In a small bowl, mix together the garlic, ginger, paprika, cumin, and olive oil. Drizzle half of this mixture over the cauliflower and sweet potato and sprinkle with a good pinch of sea salt. Mix well to coat, then cover the pan with foil and place in the oven to roast for 20 minutes.

3. Meanwhile, mix the remaining spiced oil with the okra and set aside.

4. After 20 minutes, remove the foil from the roasting pan, scatter over the okra, and season generously with sea salt. Return the pan, uncovered, to the oven for a further 20 minutes.

5. Meanwhile, mix together the yogurt and lemon juice and set aside. When the vegetables are ready, immediately drizzle on the yogurt mixture and scatter with the sliced almonds, red onion, and herbs.

SAGE-ROASTED BUTTERNUT SQUASH & MUSHROOMS WITH FETA & TOMATOES

Sage, butternut squash, and mushrooms are such a wonderful autumnal combination, and adding feta to roast along with the vegetables provides both texture and flavor. This salad is based on a recipe from my friend Emma.

Serves: 4
Prep: 10 minutes
Cook: 1 hour 5 minutes

1½ pounds [680g] butternut squash, cut into ½-inch [1.5cm] cubes
1 red onion, roughly chopped
4 cloves garlic, smashed
¾ pound [340g] cremini mushrooms, halved
4 tablespoons [60ml] olive oil
Sea salt
15 fresh sage leaves
1 cup [200g] crumbled feta cheese
¾ pound [340g] cherry tomatoes, on the vine
2 tablespoons extra-virgin olive oil
Juice of ½ lemon
1 tablespoon mustard
¼ pound [115g] arugula and watercress

1. Preheat the oven to 425°F [220°C]. Place the squash, red onion, garlic, and mushrooms in a roasting pan or large baking dish. Add the olive oil, sea salt, and half of the sage leaves and mix well. Transfer to the oven to roast for 50 minutes.

2. Give the vegetables a stir, then scatter with the feta cheese. Top wtih the cherry tomatoes and the rest of the sage leaves. Return to the oven and cook for a further 15 minutes, until the squash is soft and the tomatoes are just about to fall apart.

3. Meanwhile, mix together the extra-virgin olive oil, lemon juice, mustard, and sea salt to taste. When the vegetables are ready, dress the arugula and watercress and serve alongside.

SUMMERY ROASTED ZUCCHINI, EGGPLANT & TOMATOES WITH FETA & PINE NUTS

This summery dish, suggested by the book's lovely editor, Rowan, is as perfect for picnic antipasti as it is hot out of the oven. Lightly roasted feta is a revelation, and brings the flavors of the dish together in pleasing savoriness.

Serves: 4
Prep: 10 minutes
Cook: 45 minutes

1 eggplant, thinly sliced
2 zucchini, thinly sliced
5 ounces [140g] baby bell
  peppers, seeded and halved
2 bay leaves
2 sprigs of fresh oregano,
  leaves only
2 sprigs of fresh rosemary,
  leaves only
3 tablespoons olive oil
2 teaspoons sea salt
Freshly ground black pepper
5 vine-ripened tomatoes,
  quartered
1 cup [120g] crumbled feta
  cheese
¼ cup [30g] pine nuts
Juice of ½ lemon

Note: If baby bell peppers are not available, use a regular red or yellow bell pepper, seeded and thinly sliced.

1. Preheat the oven to 425°F [220°C]. Combine the eggplant, zucchini, peppers, bay leaves, oregano, rosemary, olive oil, sea salt, and a good grind of black pepper on a rimmed baking sheet and mix well with your hands.

2. Transfer to the oven and roast for 30 minutes, then mix in the quartered tomatoes. Scatter over the feta and pine nuts and return to the oven for a further 15 minutes.

3. Taste and season with the lemon juice and with more salt and pepper as needed before serving.

OVEN-BAKED ASPARAGUS & PARMESAN TORTILLA

Proper Spanish tortillas require long, slow cooking for the onions and potatoes, which means they're ideally suited to an oven version. I like a combination of sweet and regular potatoes for this dish, which is finished with asparagus.

Serves: 4
Prep: 10 minutes
Cook: 1 hour

1 pound [455g] potatoes, very thinly sliced
½ pound [230g] sweet potatoes, very thinly sliced
1 yellow onion, very thinly sliced
2 tablespoons olive oil
Sea salt and freshly ground black pepper
4 teaspoons [15g] finely chopped fresh tarragon
5 eggs
3 tablespoons [50g] crème fraîche
½ bunch asparagus, trimmed
1 cup [30g] grated Parmesan cheese

1. Preheat your oven to 375°F [190°C]. Place the potatoes, sweet potatoes, and onion in a small, deep roasting pan, and mix well with the olive oil, 1 teaspoon sea salt, a good grind of black pepper, and the tarragon. Cover tightly with foil, then transfer to the oven and bake for 30 minutes.

2. Meanwhile, whisk the eggs with the crème fraîche. Season well with sea salt and freshly ground black pepper. Once the potatoes and onions have had 30 minutes in the oven, pour the egg mixture all over them. Scatter over the asparagus and press the spears down a bit into the egg and potato and spinkle with the Parmesan.

3. Return the pan uncovered to the oven and bake for a further 25 to 30 minutes, until the eggs are just set. Serve hot or cold.

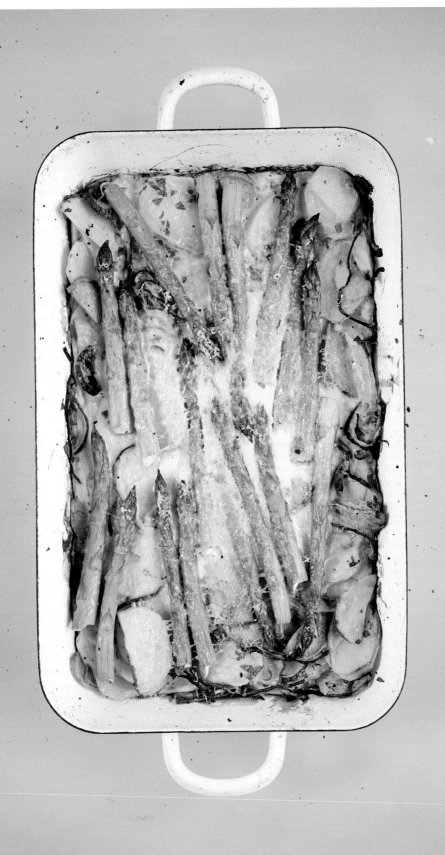

RAS EL HANOUT SLOW-ROASTED MUSHROOMS WITH PINE NUTS, HALLOUMI & PARSLEY

These mushrooms are as good as part of a vegetarian feast as they are an antipasti—and, of course, if you're building a non-vegetarian feast, they go wonderfully alongside the slow-roasted harissa lamb on page 102.

Serves: 4
Prep: 10 minutes
Cook: 1 hour 20 minutes

5 tablespoons [70g] butter
4 teaspoons ras el hanout
Zest and juice of 1 lemon
4 cloves garlic, smashed
1⅓ pounds [600g] cremini
  mushrooms
11 ounces [310g] whole shallots,
  halved
Sea salt and freshly ground
  black pepper
9 ounces [255g] halloumi
  cheese, cut into ⅜-inch
  [1cm] cubes
¼ cup [30g] pine nuts
Large handful of flat-leaf
  parsley, roughly chopped
2 teaspoons pink peppercorns
 (optional but very nice)

1. Preheat your oven to 300°F [150°C]. Place the butter, ras el hanout, lemon zest, and garlic in a roasting pan or large baking dish, then transfer to the oven for 5 minutes to melt the butter and allow the spices to toast a little.

2. Meanwhile, trim the mushrooms and peel the shallots. After the butter mixture has been in the oven for 5 minutes, pop the mushrooms and shallots into the pan, season well with sea salt and freshly ground black pepper, and mix everything together really well with your hands. Cover with foil, then place in the oven to cook for 1 hour.

3. After 1 hour, increase the heat to 325°F [170°C] and remove the foil. Sprinkle on the lemon juice, add the halloumi, and mix well before scattering on the pine nuts. Return to the oven to cook uncovered for a further 15 minutes.

4. Taste and adjust the salt as needed, and scatter on the parsley and, if you like, pink peppercorns just before serving.

QUICK & SLOW ROASTS

THESE SIMPLE ALL-IN-ONE ROASTS ARE PERFECT FOR SUBSTANTIAL WEEKNIGHT DINNERS OR TO FEED A CROWD.

4 QUICK & SLOW ROASTS

CHOOSE YOUR MEAT

SAUSAGE

LAMB

BEEF

PORK

BRISKET

CHICKEN

SEE PAGE 85 FOR
ROASTING TIMES

ADD VEGETABLES

RED BELL
PEPPER

YELLOW BELL
PEPPER

TOMATO

EGGPLANT

BUTTERNUT
SQUASH

SWEET POTATO

ADD AROMATICS + OILS

SCALLION

GARLIC

RED ONION

SALT & OILS

SEA SALT

OLIVE OIL

SESAME OIL

ADD FLAVORINGS

SPICY

BLACK PEPPER   SMOKED PAPRIKA   STAR ANISE

HARISSA   CHILE   GINGER

CUMIN   CHINESE 5 SPICE

SHARP

LEMON   LIME

WHITE WINE VINEGAR

+

ADD DAIRY + CARBS

YOGURT

GOAT CHEESE

CHEDDAR

SOUR CREAM

CARBS

COUSCOUS

FLATBREAD

TORTILLA

+

ADD GREENS + HERBS

SPINACH

HERBS

ROSEMARY   PARSLEY

OREGANO   CILANTRO

TARRAGON   THYME

MINT

ROASTING TIMES FOR MEAT

MEAT	OVEN TEMPERATURE	SUGGESTED TIME
BEEF STEAK (cut into ½-inch [1.5cm] slices)	**BROILER** Stir halfway through	**8 MINUTES** medium-well **6 MINUTES** rare
LAMB SIRLOIN STEAKS (6 ounces [170g] whole)	**BROILER** Turn halfway through	**8 MINUTES** well done
BONELESS PORK CHOPS (6 ounces [170g])	**425°F [220°C]**	**20 TO 25 MINUTES**
SAUSAGES	**400°F [200°C]**	**45 MINUTES**
LEG OF LAMB (5½ pounds [2.5kg])	**300°F [150°C]**	**3 HOURS** covered
BEEF BRISKET (2¼ pounds [1kg] plus)	**300°F [150°C]**	**3 HOURS** covered
PORK SHOULDER (3¼ pounds [1.5kg] plus)	**300°F [150°C]**	**3 HOURS** covered

FLASH-BROILED SPICED STEAK WITH PEPPERS, CHILE & ONION

These super-quick fajitas are perfect for a weeknight dinner in a hurry. Bring the roasting pan to the table and assemble them as you go.

Serves: 2
Prep: 10 to 15 minutes
Cook: 7 to 8 minutes

½ pound [230g] beef sirloin steak, cut into ¼-inch [.5cm] slices
1 fresh red chile, finely sliced
1 red bell pepper, seeded and finely sliced
1 yellow bell pepper, seeded and finely sliced
1 red onion, thinly sliced
2 teaspoons paprika
2 teaspoons ground cumin
2 teaspoons ground coriander
3 tablespoons olive oil
A good pinch of sea salt and freshly ground black pepper
4 to 6 tortillas
A large handful of fresh cilantro, roughly chopped
⅔ cup [150ml] sour cream
Lime wedges and grated cheese (optional)

Note: The steak in this recipe is cooked through. For rare steak, broil for 6 minutes in total, stirring halfway.

1. Preheat the broiler to its highest setting.

2. In a large roasting pan, mix together the steak slices, chile, bell peppers, onion, spices, olive oil, salt, and pepper. Place under the boiler and cook for 4 minutes. Meanwhile, wrap the tortillas in foil.

3. Remove the pan from the oven, give everything a good mix, then return to the broiler for a further 3 to 4 minutes, until the steak is just cooked through.

4. Remove the pan from the oven, place the foil-wrapped tortillas on a rack in the oven, and turn off the broiler. Leave the steak and vegetables to rest for 3 minutes, then scatter over the chopped cilantro and drizzle on the sour cream. Pile into the warmed tortillas and serve with lime wedges and grated cheese if you like.

CHARBROILED LAMB ON FLATBREADS WITH PINE NUTS, RAISINS & GOAT CHEESE

This is an homage to the incredibly delicious from-scratch flatbread in Ruby Tandoh's book *Flavor,* which, if you have more time than hunger, you should definitely go to. The combination of lamb and raisins is heavenly, so if you are in too much of a hurry to make your own bread, try this version with store-bought flatbreads and quick-cooking lamb sirloin steaks.

Serves: 2
Prep: 15 minutes
Cook: 8 to 12 minutes

2 lamb sirloin steaks (approx.
  6 ounces [170g] each)
2 tablespoons olive oil
1 clove garlic, minced
1 teaspoon ground cumin
1 teaspoon sea salt
A good grind of black pepper
1 yellow onion, thinly sliced
⅓ cup [50g] raisins
¼ cup [35g] pine nuts
2 flatbreads
¼ cup [60g] Greek yogurt
2 handfuls of baby spinach
⅔ cup [75g] crumbled goat
  cheese
Pomegranate seeds, to serve
  (optional)

Note: You will need a cast-iron griddle or heavy-bottomed roasting pan.

1. Preheat your broiler to the highest setting and pop in a cast-iron griddle to heat up.

2. Put the lamb steaks on a large plate and rub with the olive oil, garlic, cumin, sea salt, and freshly ground black pepper. Set the steaks to one side of the plate, then mix the sliced onion and the raisins with the oil mixture remaining on the plate.

3. After 5 minutes under the broiler, your griddle should be extremely hot—carefully remove it from the oven, place the lamb steaks on one side and the onions on the other, then return to the broiler. Cook for 6 minutes on each side for well done, or for 4 minutes on each side for medium, flipping the steaks and stirring the onions and raisins halfway through. One minute before the steaks are ready, scatter on the pine nuts and put the flatbreads on a rack in the bottom of the oven.

4. When the steaks are ready, remove them to a plate to rest for 5 minutes. Slice the steaks and season with salt and pepper as needed.

5. Spread the warm flatbreads with the yogurt and scatter over the spinach, onions, raisins, pine nuts, goat cheese, and sliced steak. Sprinkle with pomegranate seeds, if you like, and serve immediately.

FIVE-SPICE PORK CHOPS WITH ROASTED SWEET POTATOES, GINGER & GARLIC

If you travel through China, one of the nicest things you can buy from a streetside stall is a hot, roasted sweet potato. They go beautifully with garlic and ginger, and are a perfect complement to these five-spice pork chops.

Serves: 2
Prep: 10 minutes
Cook: 40 to 45 minutes

1⅓ pounds [600g] sweet potatoes, cut into ⅜-inch [1cm] cubes
2 cloves garlic, minced
2 inches [5cm] ginger, minced
1 star anise
3 tablespoons sesame oil
Sea salt
2 boneless pork chops
2 teaspoons Chinese five-spice powder
3 scallions, thinly sliced
Soy sauce, to taste

Note: If you fancy a green alongside, quarter some choy sum (Chinese flowering cabbage) or baby bok choy, toss with a little sesame oil, then chuck into the roasting pan for the last 5 to 7 minutes.

1. Preheat the oven to 425°F [220°C]. Mix the sweet potato chunks in a roasting pan or large baking dish with the garlic, ginger, star anise, 2 tablespoons of the sesame oil, and 1 teaspoon sea salt, then transfer to the oven and roast for 20 minutes.

2. Meanwhile, rub the pork chops all over with the five-spice powder, 1 teaspoon sea salt, and the remaining 1 tablespoon sesame oil. Once the sweet potatoes have had 20 minutes in the oven, pop the pork chops on top, return to the oven, and roast for 20 to 25 minutes at 400°F [200°C] until the pork is cooked to your liking.

3. Scatter over the sliced scallions, and season with soy sauce to taste.

SMOKY SAUSAGE, SWEET POTATOES & RED ONIONS

One of the easiest and most satisfying dishes in the book. Paprika gives it a wonderful smokiness, but you could easily use a combination of honey and mustard as an alternative.

Serves: 4
Prep: 10 minutes
Cook: 50 minutes

8 to 12 good-quality fresh pork sausages (approx. 1¾ pounds [800g] total)
3 sweet potatoes, peeled and cut into chunky wedges
2 red onions, cut into eighths
6 cloves garlic
4 teaspoons smoked paprika
A good splash of olive oil
Sea salt and freshly ground black pepper

1. Preheat your oven to 400°F [200°C].

2. In a roasting pan, toss the sausages, sweet potato wedges, red onions, garlic, and smoked paprika with the olive oil. Season well with sea salt and freshly ground black pepper.

3. Transfer to the oven and roast for 45 to 50 minutes, until the sweet potatoes are cooked through and the sausages are sticky and slightly charred. Serve immediately.

LEMON AND ROSEMARY STEAK WITH GARLIC-ROASTED POTATOES & RED ONION

Here, a quick flash in a scorchingly hot pan before finishing the steaks on top of the potatoes in the oven gives a far superior flavor and appearance than just oven-roasting. The steaks are marinated after cooking in a lemon and rosemary dressing.

Serves: 2
Prep: 15 minutes
Cook: 1 hour 10 minutes

1⅓ pounds [600g] potatoes, cut into ⅜-inch [1cm] cubes
1 red onion, roughly sliced
2 cloves garlic, smashed
4 tablespoons olive oil
Sea salt
2 or 3 sprigs of fresh rosemary, plus leaves of 3 sprigs, finely chopped
Two ½ pound [230g] beef sirloin steaks, at least ¾ inch [2cm] thick
Freshly ground black pepper
Zest and juice of ½ lemon
3 tablespoons extra-virgin olive oil

1. Preheat your oven to 400°F [200°C]. Mix the potatoes, onion, garlic, 2 tablespoons of the olive oil, 1 heaping teaspoon sea salt, and the rosemary sprigs in a roasting pan or large baking dish, then transfer to the oven and roast for 40 minutes. When the potatoes have had 20 minutes in the oven, remove the steaks from the fridge and place on a plate. Rub all over with the remaining 2 tablespoons olive oil and season with freshly ground black pepper. Set aside to come to room temperature.

2. Once the potatoes have have cooked for 40 minutes, turn up the oven temperature to 425°F [220°C] and continue to roast until they are nice and crisp and golden, a further 20 minutes.

3. Meanwhile, combine the chopped rosemary, lemon zest and juice, the extra-virgin olive oil, and 1 teaspoon sea salt and set aside.

4. When the potatoes are done, warm a griddle or heavy-bottomed skillet over high heat until smoking. Season the steaks with a little sea salt, then place on the griddle or in the pan for 1½ minutes, flipping them halfway through, until they are nicely browned on both sides.

5. Transfer the steaks to the oven on top of the potatoes and roast for a further 2 minutes for rare, 4½ minutes for medium-rare, or 6 to 8 minutes for well done.

6. Remove the roasting pan from the oven and place the steaks on a plate. Pour on the dressing, then cover with foil and leave to rest for 5 to 6 minutes. Slice and serve with the potatoes.

SLOW-COOKED BRISKET WITH CHIMICHURRI

A Sunday roast with a twist. The sharp, Argentinean parsley sauce is a wonderful and unusual accompaniment to the meat and vegetables.

Serves: 4
Prep: 10 minutes
Cook: 3 hours

1 teaspoon red pepper flakes
Zest of 1 lemon
2 cloves garlic, smashed
Leaves of 6 sprigs fresh oregano, finely chopped
2 teaspoons sea salt
3 tablespoons olive oil
2¼ pounds [1kg] lean beef brisket, from the thin end
1⅓ pounds [600g] butternut squash, cut into 1¼-inch [3cm] chunks
1 red onion, quartered
1¾ cups [420ml] chicken stock
7 tablespoons [100ml] white wine vinegar

CHIMICHURRI
¾ cup [30g] finely chopped fresh flat-leaf parsley
1 fresh red chile, finely chopped
1 clove garlic, finely chopped
5 tablespoons olive oil
3 tablespoons white wine vinegar
Sea salt

1. Preheat the oven to 300°F [150°C]. Mix together the red pepper flakes, lemon zest, garlic, oregano, salt, and olive oil, then rub this mixture all over the brisket. Roll the brisket so the meat's fibers run the length of the roll and tie securely with twine.

2. Add the butternut squash, red onion, chicken stock, and white wine vinegar to a roasting pan or large baking dish and put the beef on top. Cover tightly with foil, then place in the oven and cook for 3 hours.

3. Meanwhile, make the chimichurri. Mix the parsley, chile, and garlic with the olive oil and white wine vinegar and season to taste with sea salt.

4. Slice the brisket, then serve with the butternut squash and the chimichurri alongside.

FILIPINO-STYLE GARLIC PORK POT ROAST

This unusual pork pot roast uses the classic Filipino adobo flavors of garlic, bay leaf, peppercorns, and vinegar to slow-cook a whole pork shoulder. For a lazy weekend lunch, it's a win—ten minutes in the morning to sear off the pork and garlic before sticking everything in the oven and letting it bubble away until lunchtime.

Serves: 5 or 6
Prep: 10 minutes
Cook: 2 hours 50 minutes

2 tablespoons vegetable oil
3¼ pounds [1.5kg] boneless pork shoulder roast
1 head garlic, halved horizontally
3 bay leaves
1 teaspoon whole black peppercorns
2½ cups [600ml] chicken stock
2 tablespoons soy sauce, plus more to serve
3½ tablespoons rice or white wine vinegar
1¾ cups [340g] basmati rice, rinsed
6 baby bok choy, halved or quartered if large
Sea salt

1. Preheat the oven to 300°F [150°C].

2. Heat the vegetable oil in a large Dutch oven over medium-high heat and sear the pork shoulder for 3 minutes on each side, until well browned all over.

3. Move the pork to one side of the pot, then add the two halves of the garlic head, cut-side down, along with the bay leaves and peppercorns, and cook for a minute.

4. Pour in the chicken stock, soy sauce, and vinegar and bring to a boil, then immediately cover, transfer to the oven, and cook for 1 hour and 45 minutes. Add the rice and cook for a further 45 minutes, then add the baby bok choy and cook for a further 10 minutes.

5. Using a couple of spoons, pull the pork apart into large chunks. Serve with the bok choy and rice alongside, seasoning to taste with soy sauce or sea salt.

SLOW-COOKED LEG OF LAMB WITH HARISSA, ROASTED EGGPLANTS & TOMATOES

Lamb is robust enough to stand up to strong flavors, and this Middle Eastern–inspired leg of lamb with a harissa kick really delivers. Perfect to feed a crowd.

Serves: 8
Prep: 15 minutes
Cook: 3 hours

2 eggplants, cut into ½-inch [1.5cm] rounds
1 red onion, sliced
4½- to 5½-pound [2 to 2.5kg] leg of lamb
1 head garlic, halved horizontally
4 heaping teaspoons harissa paste
1 tablespoon sea salt
1 tablespoon olive oil
12 ounces [340g] tomatoes on the vine
2 handfuls couscous (optional)
1 cup [250g] Greek yogurt
1 bunch of fresh mint, leaves finely chopped

1. Preheat the oven to 300°F [150°C]. Line a roasting pan with the eggplant slices, then scatter over the onion. Place the leg of lamb on top of the vegetables and tuck the garlic halves alongside.

2. Stab the lamb all over with a very sharp knife, then rub all over with the harissa paste. Sprinkle the meat and vegetables with the sea salt, then drizzle the oil over the garlic and vegetables. Transfer to the oven and roast, uncovered, for 30 minutes then cover with foil and roast for a further 1 hour and 30 minutes.

3. Then add the tomatoes to the pan, cover, and return the lamb to the oven for a final 1 hour. Throw in the couscous (if using) to cook in the juices in the roasting pan for the last 10 minutes.

4. Meanwhile, mix together the Greek yogurt and mint.

5. Allow the lamb to rest for at least 15 minutes before serving with the couscous, vegetables, and yogurt.

TARRAGON ROASTED CHICKEN WITH POTATOES, ONIONS & GARLIC

This roast chicken cooks above the potatoes in the style of a French rotisserie chicken (if more static). Tarragon provides another nod to French flavors—you need little alongside this other than perhaps a little of the mustard mayonnaise on page 44.

Serves: 6
Prep: 15 minutes
Cook: 2 hours

2¾ pounds [1.3kg] new potatoes, fingerlings, or other small roasting potatoes
5 tablespoons [20g] chopped fresh tarragon
1 head garlic, halved horizontally
6 strips of zest from 1 lemon
2 tablespoons olive oil
Sea salt and freshly ground black pepper
5-pound [2.3kg] whole chicken
2 tablespoons butter

1. Preheat the oven to 350F° [180°C]. Place the potatoes, half of the tarragon, 1 half of the garlic head, the lemon zest strips, and the olive oil in a roasting pan and mix well with your hands. Season with a really generous amount of sea salt and freshly ground black pepper.

2. Place the chicken on top of the potato mixture. Cut the lemon in half and stuff the halves in the chicken along with the other half of the tarragon and the remaining half of the garlic. Rub the chicken all over with the butter, then season really generously with sea salt and freshly ground black pepper.

3. Place in the oven and roast for 1½ hours, then turn up the temperature to 400°F [200°C] and cook until the chicken skin and the potatoes are crisp, another 30 minutes.

4. Let the chicken rest under foil for 10 to 15 minutes before serving.

RICE & PASTA

FOR EXTRA CARBS, FIRE UP A PAN OF BOILING WATER—YOUR RICE OR PASTA WILL BE READY JUST AS THE DINNER COMES OUT OF THE OVEN.

5 RICE & PASTA

CHOOSE YOUR RICE OR PASTA

BROWN RICE

BASMATI RICE

JASMINE RICE

WILD RICE

RISOTTO RICE
(CARNAROLI, ARBORIO)

RED RICE
(CAMARGUE, HIMALAYAN)

PASTA

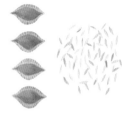

CONCHIGLIETTE   ORZO   GNOCCHI

FUSILLI

RIGATONI

SEE PAGE 111 FOR ROASTING TIMES

ADD PROTEIN OR CHEESE

CHICKEN

TUNA

SEA BASS

SALMON

PANCETTA

SAUSAGE

EGGS

FETA

GOAT CHEESE

MOZZARELLA

PARMESAN

ROQUEFORT

ADD VEGETABLES

AVOCADO   BEET   FENNEL

ASPARAGUS   SCALLION   BRUSSELS SPROUTS

MUSHROOM

EGGPLANT   TOMATO   ARTICHOKES

BROCCOLI   POTATO   RED BELL PEPPER

FLAVORINGS

GARLIC   LIME   LEMON   CHILE   GINGER

ADD TOPPINGS

PINE NUTS   HAZELNUTS   WALNUTS

POMEGRANATE   YOGURT   MANGO

GREENS

BABY BOK CHOY   ARUGULA   SPINACH

KALE

HERBS

BASIL   CILANTRO   MINT

COOKING TIMES FOR RICE & PASTA

RICE/PASTA	OVEN TEMPERATURE	SUGGESTED TIME
MIXED BASMATI & WILD RICE (1 cup [200g] rice plus 1½ cups [360ml] water or stock)	350°F [180°C]	**40 MINUTES** covered **10 MINUTES** uncovered
BROWN RICE (1½ cups [300g] rice plus 3¼ cups [750ml] water or stock)	400°F [200°C]	**1 HOUR** covered
RISOTTO RICE (1½ cups [300g] rice plus 6⅓ cups [1.5 liters] stock)	350°F [180°C]	**50 MINUTES** covered
ORZO (1½ cups [250g] orzo plus 2⅛ cups [500ml] stock)	425°F [220°C]	**15 TO 20 MINUTES** covered

OR BOIL IN SALTED WATER

Drain well, then return to the pan and leave rice covered to steam dry for 5 minutes.

JASMINE RICE	**15 MINUTES**
BASMATI RICE	**15 MINUTES**
BROWN RICE	**30 MINUTES**
MIXED BASMATI & WILD RICE	**25 TO 30 MINUTES**
RED RICE	**35 TO 40 MINUTES**
PASTA	See package instructions

MISO ROAST SALMON WITH MUSHROOMS, BOK CHOY & JASMINE RICE

Savory miso, with its deep umami flavor, beautifully complements the salmon in this dish, while the bok choy cuts through the richness. And because this dish can be made from start to finish in 25 minutes, it's well worth keeping a container of miso paste in the fridge for quick-fix dinners.

Serves: 2
Prep: 5 minutes
Cook: 20 minutes

1 cup [200g] jasmine rice
2 salmon fillets
½ pound [230g] wild mushrooms, roughly chopped
2 large baby bok choy, quartered
2 cloves garlic, grated
2 inches [5cm] ginger, grated
2 tablespoons [30g] miso paste
4 teaspoons [20ml] rice vinegar

1. Preheat the oven to 400°F [200°C]. Add the rice to a pot of boiling salted water and simmer for 15 minutes, until cooked through, then drain in a sieve. Return the rice to the pot, cover, and allow to steam dry for 5 minutes.

2. Meanwhile, arrange the salmon fillets, mushrooms, and bok choy in a roasting pan or large baking dish. Mix the garlic and ginger with the miso paste and rice vinegar, and spread 1 teaspoon of this mixture on each salmon fillet. Dollop the remaining mixture over the bok choy and mushrooms.

3. Cover tightly with foil, then transfer to the oven to roast for 20 minutes.

4. Serve the hot salmon and vegetables with the rice alongside.

SEA BASS, ASPARAGUS & SCALLIONS WITH JASMINE RICE & GINGER, LIME & SOY DRESSING

A light, Southeast Asian–inspired dressing is the perfect complement to the simple roasted sea bass and greens in this dish—a perfectly balanced meal along with a pot of fluffy white rice.

Serves: 2
Prep: 10 minutes
Cook: 15 minutes

1 cup [200g] jasmine rice
¼ pound [115g] asparagus
½ pound [230g] baby bok choy, quartered
1 tablespoon peanut oil
2 sea bass fillets
1½ inches [4cm] ginger, grated
2 cloves garlic, grated
1 fresh red chile, thinly sliced
1 scallion, thinly sliced
3 tablespoons sesame oil
Zest and juice of 1 lime
1 tablespoon fish sauce
1 tablespoon soy sauce
A small handful of fresh cilantro, finely chopped

1. Preheat the oven to 400°F [200°C]. Add the rice to a pot of boiling salted water and simmer for 15 minutes, until cooked through, then drain in a sieve. Return the rice to the pot, cover, and allow to steam dry for 5 minutes.

2. Meanwhile, place the asparagus and bok choy in a roasting pan or large baking dish and toss with the peanut oil. Transfer to the preheated oven and roast for 5 minutes, then place the sea bass fillets on top and return the pan to the oven for a further 8 minutes.

3. Mix the ginger, garlic, red chile, and scallion with the sesame oil, lime zest and juice, fish sauce, soy sauce, and cilantro. Drizzle the dressing over the cooked fish and greens and serve immediately, with the rice alongside.

AVOCADO & CHICKEN SALAD WITH POMEGRANATES & BROWN RICE

This simple chicken salad provides a wonderful contrast of flavors and textures. Baked avocado might sound odd, but it's so delicious, particularly when paired with crisp pomegranate seeds and chile-spiked chicken. It's more filling than it looks, so it will serve four people as a light main or two hungrier people—by all means, scale up the chicken and avocado depending on your audience.

Serves: 2 to 4
Prep: 10 minutes
Cook: 30 minutes

1½ cups [300g] brown rice
2 avocados
2 large boneless, skinless
  chicken breasts
1 teaspoon red pepper flakes
Sea salt and freshly ground
  black pepper
3 tablespoons olive oil
Juice of 2 limes
6 tablespoons extra-virgin
  olive oil
½ cup [30g] finely chopped
  fresh mint leaves
Seeds of 2 pomegranates
½ pound [230g] baby spinach,
  finely chopped

1. Preheat your oven to 400°F [200°C]. Add the rice to a large pot of boiling salted water and simmer for 30 minutes, until the rice is cooked through but ever so slightly al dente, then drain in a sieve. Return the rice to the pot, cover, and allow to steam dry for 5 minutes.

   Meanwhile, halve the avocados and
2. remove the pits, then place them face up in a roasting pan or large baking dish along with the chicken breasts, making sure everything is in one layer. Scatter over the red pepper flakes, sea salt, and freshly ground black pepper and drizzle with the olive oil. Mix everything briefly until well coated with the oil, then pop the roasting pan into the oven for 25 minutes, until the chicken is cooked through.

3. For the dressing, whisk together the lime juice, extra-virgin olive oil, mint, and pomegranate seeds, then season with salt and pepper and set aside.

4. Remove the cooked chicken and avocados from the roasting pan and slice them, discarding the avocado skin. Add the cooked rice to the pan along with half of the dressing and all of the spinach, and mix them well with the oil left in the pan. Lay the cooked chicken and avocado on top, drizzle on the remaining dressing, and serve.

WILD RICE WINTER SALAD WITH ROASTED BRUSSELS SPROUTS, PANCETTA, FETA & SUNFLOWER SEEDS

Brussels sprouts and pancetta are a classic pairing for a reason—they're utterly compelling together. Carbed up with some wild rice, with seeds for crunch and feta and lemon for flavor, this rice salad is as lovely for a hot dinner as it is for a cold lunch the next day.

Serves: 2 generously
Prep: 10 minutes
Cook: 30 minutes

1 cup [200g] mixed basmati and wild rice
1 pound [455g] Brussels sprouts, halved
3 ounces [80g] pancetta, cubed
Sea salt and freshly ground black pepper
2 tablespoons olive oil
⅓ cup [50g] shelled sunflower seeds
Juice of 1 lemon
¾ cup [100g] crumbled feta cheese
A handful of fresh flat-leaf parsley, finely chopped

1. Preheat the oven to 400°F [200°C]. Add the rice to a pot of boiling salted water and simmer for 25 to 30 minutes, until cooked through, then drain in a sieve. Return the rice to the pot, cover, and allow to steam dry for 5 minutes.

2. Meanwhile, place the sprouts and pancetta in a roasting pan or baking dish large enough to hold them in a single layer. Season well with sea salt and freshly ground black pepper and drizzle with the olive oil, working everything together with your hands. Place in the oven and roast for 25 to 30 minutes. Throw in the sunflower seeds for the final 5 minutes of cooking.

3. Stir the rice into the roasted sprouts and pancetta along with the lemon juice, crumbled feta, and parsley. Taste and season as needed with sea salt and black pepper and serve hot.

SESAME & GINGER MEATBALLS WITH BOK CHOY, CHILE & RED RICE

Sesame and ginger were made to go with meatballs. These beauties are pepped up with a subtle chile kick, and you will find that oven roasting gives them a lovely texture. Use all ground beef, a mixture of beef and pork, or lamb if you prefer. These are best eaten straight from the oven.

Serves: 4
Prep: 15 minutes
Cook: 35 to 40 minutes

1 cup [200g] red rice, rinsed
1 pound [455g] good-quality
  ground beef
3 scallions, very thinly sliced
½ fresh red chile, seeded and
  finely chopped
2 inches [5cm] ginger, grated
1 clove garlic, grated
2 tablespoons sesame oil
1 tablespoon sesame seeds
1 teaspoon sea salt
4 baby bok choy, cut into
  eighths

DRESSING
1 inch [2.5cm] ginger, grated
1 clove garlic, grated
2 tablespoons sesame oil
Zest and juice of 1 lime
2 scallions, sliced
½ fresh red chile, seeded and
  sliced
1 teaspoon sea salt

1. Preheat the oven to 400°F [200°C]. Add the rice to a pot of boiling salted water and simmer for 35 to 40 minutes, until cooked through.

2. Meanwhile, in a large bowl, work together the ground beef, scallions, chile, ginger, grated garlic, sesame oil, sesame seeds, and sea salt until completely blended, then form into twenty-four walnut-size balls. Pop them into a roasting pan or large baking dish and roast in the oven for 25 minutes, until cooked through and golden brown.

3. Meanwhile, mix together all the dressing ingredients and set aside.

4. Once the meatballs have had 25 minutes in the oven, tuck the bok choy into the roasting pan, and return to the oven for a further 5 to 6 minutes, until the bok choy is wilted.

5. When the rice is done, drain it in a sieve and add it to the pan with the meatballs and bok choy. Pour over the dressing and mix well before serving.

FIVE-SPICE DUCK BREASTS WITH WILD RICE, KALE & GINGER

This incredibly satisfying duck and wild rice dish, with its contrast of complementary textures and flavors, is easily scaled up if you're cooking for more than two. Probably one of my favorite recipes in the book.

Serves: 2
Prep: 10 minutes
Cook: 50 minutes

1 cup [200g] mixed basmati
    and wild rice
1½ cups [350ml] water
2 inches [5cm] ginger, grated
2 cloves garlic, whole
2 teaspoons sea salt
1 star anise
½ bunch kale, destemmed and
    roughly chopped
1 tablespoon sesame oil
2 duck breasts (approx.
    ¾ pound [340g] each)
2 teaspoons Chinese five-spice
    powder
½ fresh red chile, thinly sliced
2 scallions, thinly sliced

1. Preheat your oven to 350°F [180°C]. Mix the rice, water, ginger, garlic, and 1 teaspoon of the sea salt in a roasting pan or large baking dish, and throw in the star anise.

2. Mix the kale with the sesame oil, then scatter it over the rice.

3. Slash the skin on the duck breasts with a sharp knife, then rub them all over with the remaining 1 teaspoon sea salt and the five-spice powder. Place on top of the kale, cover the roasting pan tightly with foil, then transfer to the oven and roast for 40 minutes.

4. Remove the foil and cook uncovered for a further 10 minutes, to allow the kale to crisp up. Allow the duck breasts to rest for 5 minutes, then thinly slice and return the breasts to the roasting pan. Scatter over the red chile and scallions and serve.

SPICED ROASTED EGGPLANTS & POTATOES WITH COCONUT BASMATI RICE, YOGURT & CILANTRO

This is my version of a favorite South Indian dish, where eggplants and potatoes are mixed with oil and sambar powder (the seasoning for a type of dhal made there). The vegetables are then roasted until crisp, in my mother's version, and sprinkled with plenty of salt. Most of this gets stolen straight from the roasting pan.

Serves: 4
Prep: 10 minutes
Cook: 1 hour

2 eggplants
1 pound [455g] potatoes
2 teaspoons ground coriander
2 teaspoons ground cumin
½ teaspoon pure spicy chile
   powder (1 teaspoon if not
   very spicy)
Sea salt
3 tablespoons vegetable oil
1½ cups [300g] basmati rice,
   rinsed
One 14.5-ounce [400ml] can of
   coconut milk
1½ cups [350ml] water
¼ cup [60g] Greek yogurt
½ cup [15g] fresh cilantro leaves

1. Preheat the oven to 400°F [200°C]. Halve the eggplants and potatoes lengthwise, then cut the eggplants into ⅜-inch [1cm] half-moons and the potatoes into ¼-inch [.5cm] half-moons. Transfer to a very large roasting pan or a rimmed baking sheet.

2. Mix together the ground coriander, cumin, chile powder, and 1 teaspoon sea salt, then scatter all over the potatoes and eggplants. Drizzle with the vegetable oil, then mix everything together with your hands. Transfer to the oven to roast for 1 hour.

3. Place the rinsed rice, coconut milk, and water in a saucepan with a tight-fitting lid, add a pinch of salt, and stir well. Bring to a boil, stir, then replace the lid and simmer over low heat for 15 minutes. Remove the lid, fluff the rice, replace the lid, and leave to dry steam for a further 5 minutes.

4. Taste and season the cooked eggplants and potatoes. Spoon on the Greek yogurt, scatter over the cilantro, and serve immediately with the rice.

OVEN-COOKED BEET RISOTTO

A few minutes of light stirring at the beginning and this vibrantly pink risotto will look after itself in the oven. Perfect to feed a crowd.

Serves: 4 to 6
Prep: 10 minutes
Cook: 1 hour 15 minutes

2 tablespoons olive oil
1 yellow onion, finely chopped
A pinch of sea salt
1½ cups [300g] carnaroli or arborio rice
14 ounces [400g] fresh beets, grated
½ cup [120ml] white wine
6 cups [1.5L] vegetable stock
4 ounces [115g] goat cheese, crumbled
6 tablespoons [50g] skinned hazelnuts
A handful of arugula
Freshly ground black pepper

Note: You will need a casserole dish suitable to use on the stove top and in the oven.

1. Preheat the oven to 350°F [180°C]. Heat the oil in a flameproof casserole dish and add the onion and a pinch of salt. Stir briefly, then cover and leave to soften for 10 minutes, stirring once halfway through.

2. Add the rice and cook, stirring constantly, for 1 minute, then add the beets. Stir, add the white wine, and simmer for 1 minute, then add the stock. Bring to a boil, then cover and transfer to the oven for 40 minutes.

3. Uncover the casserole and top the risotto with the goat cheese and hazelnuts. Replace the cover and return to the oven for a further 10 minutes.

4. Scatter the arugula and some freshly ground black pepper over the risotto and serve immediately.

ORZO WITH CHILE & GARLIC-ROASTED BROCCOLI, LEMON, PARMESAN & WALNUTS

Orzo is one of my favorite pasta shapes, and it's particularly well suited to oven cooking. If you have any leftover rinds of Parmesan, chuck them in with the stock—they will lend the most amazing flavor to the finished dish.

Serves: 3 or 4
Prep: 15 minutes
Cook: 25 to 30 minutes

1 large head of broccoli, cut
   into small florets
1 yellow onion, finely chopped
2 tablespoons olive oil
2 cloves garlic, smashed
1 teaspoon red pepper flakes
Sea salt
1½ cups [250g] orzo
2 cups plus 2 tablespoons
   [500ml] vegetable stock
½ cup [60g] walnuts
2 ounces [60g] Parmesan
   cheese, grated
Zest and juice of ½ lemon
¼ pound [115g] baby spinach,
   roughly chopped

Note: If you know your red pepper flakes are quite hot, use ½ teaspoon.

1. Preheat the oven to 425°F [220°C]. Mix together the broccoli, onion, olive oil, garlic, red pepper flakes, and 1 teaspoon sea salt in a roasting pan or large baking dish, then transfer to the oven and roast for 10 minutes.

2. Stir in the orzo and the vegetable stock, cover carefully with foil, then return to the oven for a further 15 to 20 minutes, until the stock is absorbed. Spread the walnuts on a baking sheet and transfer to the oven for the last 5 minutes to toast.

3. Remove the foil from the roasting pan and stir in the Parmesan and lemon zest and juice. Season with more sea salt as needed. Stir in the spinach, then scatter over the toasted walnuts and serve.

CRISPY BAKED GNOCCHI WITH TOMATOES, BASIL, MOZZARELLA & PINE NUTS

This baked, unashamedly carb-loaded version of an insalata caprese is one of the quickest and easiest dinners in this book. Crispy gnocchi is a revelation—like the best roast potatoes you've ever had, but faster. Liz Taylor would have approved.

Serves: 2 as a main
(4 as a side/starter)
Prep: 10 minutes
Cook: 30 minutes

1 pound [455g] potato gnocchi
2 tablespoons olive oil
¾ pound [340g] vine-ripened tomatoes, cut into eighths
5 ounces [140g] fresh mozzarella, cut into bite-size chunks
Leaves of 1 large bunch of fresh basil
Sea salt and freshly ground black pepper
⅓ cup [40g] pine nuts

1. Preheat your oven to 425°F [220°C].

2. Place the gnocchi in a large bowl and cover with boiling water. Leave to cook for 2 minutes, then drain well.

3. Add the cooked gnocchi to a roasting pan or large baking dish along with the olive oil and mix well to evenly coat. Tuck in the tomatoes, mozzarella, and half of the basil. Season with sea salt and freshly ground black pepper, then transfer to the oven and bake for 20 minutes.

4. Scatter the pine nuts over the gnocchi and bake for a further 5 minutes.

5. Tear the rest of the basil leaves, scatter them over the gnocchi, and serve immediately.

BAKED EGG
PASTA FLORENTINE

Eggs, spinach, and nutmeg are such a comforting combination, and wonderful with pasta. Pepped up with spicy chorizo or sharp feta, this simple dish is one to pile onto plates and take to the nearest sofa.

Serves: 2
Prep: 10 minutes
Cook: 40 minutes

½ pound [230g] spaghetti
⅔ cup [150g] crème fraîche
Sea salt and freshly ground
  black pepper
Grated nutmeg
½ pound [230g] baby spinach
¼ pound [115g] roughly
  chopped Spanish chorizo or
  feta cheese
4 eggs
½ lemon

1. Preheat your oven to 325°F [170°C]. Cook the spaghetti in a pot of boiling salted water for 9 minutes, until just al dente. Drain well, reserving 2 table-spoons of the pasta water, then return the pasta to the pot and stir through the crème fraîche, the reserved pasta water, 1 teaspoon sea salt, a pinch of freshly ground black pepper, and nutmeg. Taste and add more salt as needed, but bear in mind that the chorizo or feta will also be quite salty.

2. Add the pasta to a baking dish and gradually stir through the spinach (this will seem like an impossible task, but bear with it). Congratulate yourself, then scatter over half of the chorizo or feta.

3. Make four indentations in the pasta and spinach and crack the eggs in. Scatter over the remaining chorizo or feta, sprinkle with a little more salt, freshly ground black pepper, and nutmeg onto the eggs, then transfer to the oven to bake for 25 minutes, until the eggs are just set.

4. Squeeze the juice from the lemon half onto the pasta and serve immediately.

RIGATONI AL FORNO WITH PANCETTA, ARTICHOKES, CRÈME FRAÎCHE & PARMESAN

This is my version of Niki Segnit's wonderful pancetta and artichoke pasta in *The Flavour Thesaurus*—both my favorite cookbook and my favorite pasta dish. This version has marginally less cheese and cream—I would direct you to her book for the unashamedly delicious and rib-sticking original. My amendments over the years are the result of not having enough ingredients, rather than any desire to go low-fat.

Serves: 2
Prep: 10 minutes
Cook: 40 minutes

3 ounces [80g] pancetta, cubed
One 10-ounce [280g] jar oil-packed artichokes, drained (reserve the oil)
1 white onion, finely chopped
7 ounces [200g] rigatoni
1¼ cups [300g] crème fraîche
¼ cup [10g] finely chopped fresh flat-leaf parsley
Sea salt and freshly ground black pepper
2½ ounces [75g] Parmesan cheese, grated
1 cup [50g] panko breadcrumbs

1. Preheat the oven to 425°F [220°C].

2. Mix the pancetta, drained artichokes, and white onion in a roasting pan or large baking dish, along with 1 tablespoon of the reserved artichoke oil, then transfer to the oven and roast for 20 minutes.

3. Meanwhile, bring a large pot of salted water to a boil, then add the pasta and cook until al dente, about 10 minutes. Drain the pasta well.

4. When the artichoke mixture has had 20 minutes in the oven, add the drained pasta and mix well. Stir in the crème fraîche and parsley and season with sea salt and freshly ground black pepper.

5. Scatter over the Parmesan and breadcrumbs and return to the oven for a further 20 minutes, until golden brown and crisp. Serve immediately.

FENNEL, SAUSAGE & CANNELLINI BEANS WITH TOMATOES & CONCHIGLIETTE

This rich, warming all-in-one pasta dish is perfect weekend comfort food. If you can find spicy sausages, they will go particularly well with the fennel and tomatoes.

Serves: 4
Prep: 10 minutes
Cook: 55 minutes

1 yellow onion, finely chopped
1 fennel bulb, finely chopped
10 ounces [280g] sweet Italian sausages, sliced into ½-inch [1.5cm] coins
2 tablespoons olive oil
One 28-ounce [800g] can diced tomatoes, with juice
One 14.5-ounce [400g] can cannellini beans, drained
2 cloves garlic, smashed
10½ ounces [300g] conchigliette
1 sprig of fresh rosemary
3 or 4 sprigs of fresh oregano, plus a handful of fresh oregano leaves
1 teaspoon brown sugar
Sea salt and freshly ground black pepper
2 cups plus 2 tablespoons [500ml] water
2 tablespoons extra-virgin olive oil
A handful of shaved Parmesan cheese

1. Preheat your broiler to its highest setting. Add the onion, fennel, and sausages to a roasting pan or broiler-safe baking dish along with the olive oil, and mix briefly.

2. Transfer to the broiler and cook for 10 minutes. Give everything a stir, return to the broiler for a further 5 minutes, until evenly browned, then remove.

3. Turn off the broiler, and preheat your oven to 400°F [200°C]. Add the tomatoes and their juice, cannellini beans, garlic, conchigliette, rosemary, oregano, brown sugar, 2 teaspoons sea salt, a good grind of black pepper and the water to the sausages and onions. Stir well, then return the pan to the oven for a further 40 minutes.

4. Taste and adjust the salt and pepper as needed. Stir in the extra-virgin olive oil and scatter over the oregano and Parmesan just before serving.

GOAT CHEESE, RED PEPPER, MUSHROOM & PESTO FUSILLI

This is my version of my sister Padmini's favorite roasted dish. When we were roommates, we'd cook on alternate nights, and I was always so happy to come home and find this in the oven—a lovely, filling vegetarian main.

Serves: 4
Prep: 15 minutes
Cook: 50 minutes

3 red bell peppers, seeded and roughly chopped
1 pound [455g] cremini mushrooms
3 tablespoons olive oil
4 cloves garlic, smashed
3 or 4 sprigs of fresh rosemary
Sea salt and freshly ground black pepper
½ teaspoon red pepper flakes
¾ pound [340g] fusilli
One 28-ounce [800g] can diced tomatoes, with juice
⅔ cup [150g] pesto
A good handful of grated Parmesan cheese
½ pound [230g] goat cheese, sliced

1. Preheat the oven to 425°F [220°C]. Add the bell peppers, mushrooms, olive oil, garlic, rosemary, 2 teaspoons of sea salt, freshly ground black pepper, and the red pepper flakes to a large roasting pan and mix well. Transfer to the oven and bake for 20 minutes.

2. Meanwhile, bring a large pot of salted water to a boil, and cook the fusilli until al dente, then drain well.

3. When the vegetables have had 20 minutes in the oven, add the fusilli and tomatoes with their juice to the pan along with a good couple of pinches of sea salt and mix well. Dollop on the pesto and scatter over the Parmesan and goat cheese. Return to the oven and bake for a further 30 minutes, until golden and bubbling.

SUPERGRAINS

COOKED IN THE ROASTING PAN ALONG WITH THE OTHER INGREDIENTS AND STOCK, THESE GRAINS TAKE ON LOTS OF FLAVOR WITH MINIMUM EFFORT.

6 SUPERGRAINS

CHOOSE YOUR GRAIN

QUINOA
(RED, WHITE, BLACK)

COUSCOUS
(ISRAELI, REGULAR)

PEARLED BARLEY

BULGUR WHEAT

SPELT

BUCKWHEAT

FARRO

OATS

SEE PAGE 145 FOR ROASTING TIMES

ADD VEGETABLES

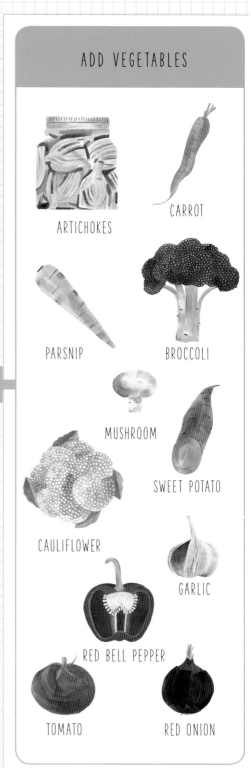

ARTICHOKES

CARROT

PARSNIP

BROCCOLI

MUSHROOM

SWEET POTATO

CAULIFLOWER

GARLIC

RED BELL PEPPER

TOMATO

RED ONION

+

ADD PROTEIN OR CHEESE

LAMB

CHORIZO

GOAT CHEESE

FETA

HALLOUMI

CHEDDAR

GORGONZOLA

PARMESAN

ADD TOPPINGS

PISTACHIOS

APRICOTS

PINE NUTS

HAZELNUTS

GREENS

BASIL

ARUGULA

SPINACH

MINT

COOKING TIMES FOR GRAINS

GRAINS	OVEN TEMPERATURE	SUGGESTED TIME
QUINOA (⅔ cup [120g] quinoa plus 1½ cups [360ml] water or stock)	425°F [220°C]	20 MINUTES covered
ISRAELI COUSCOUS (1½ cups [200g] Israeli couscous plus 1¾ cups [420ml] stock)	400°F [200°C]	20 MINUTES covered
REGULAR COUSCOUS (1 cup [200g] whole-wheat couscous plus 1 cup plus 1 tablespoon [250ml] stock)	350°F [180°C]	10 MINUTES covered
PEARLED BARLEY (¾ cup [150g] pearled barley plus 1½ cups [360ml] water or stock)	325°F [170°C] covered	1 HOUR
BULGUR WHEAT (1¼ cups [200g] bulgur wheat plus 1⅔ cups [400ml] water or stock)	400°F [200°C]	15 MINUTES covered
SPELT (¾ cup [150g] spelt plus 1½ cups [360ml] water or stock)	325°F [170°C]	1 HOUR covered
BUCKWHEAT (¾ cup [140g] buckwheat plus 1⅓ cups [320ml] water or stock)	325°F [170°C]	30 MINUTES covered
FARRO (¾ cup [150g] quick-cooking farro plus 1½ cups [360ml] water or stock)	400°F [200°C]	30 MINUTES covered

SUPER-SIMPLE SALMON À LA PESTO WITH ISRAELI COUSCOUS, WATERCRESS & LEMON

Salmon à la pesto was an absolute university staple. This version adds a quick-cooking carb in the same roasting pan so you don't have to worry about a side dish to go with it. Peppery watercress makes a great match for the salmon, but you could also use spinach or arugula.

Serves: 2
Prep: 5 minutes
Cook: 20 minutes

1½ cups [200g] Israeli whole-wheat couscous
1⅔ cups [400ml] vegetable stock
Zest and juice of 2 lemons
2 skinless salmon fillets, (approx. 7 ounces [200g] each)
2 tablespoons of your favorite pesto
2½ tablespoons [20g] pine nuts, roughly chopped
3½ ounces [100g] watercress, roughly chopped
Sea salt and freshly ground black pepper

1. Preheat the oven to 400°F [200°C]. Add the couscous to a roasting pan or large baking dish along with the vegetable stock and lemon zest.

2. Place the salmon fillets on top of the couscous and spread the pesto over the fillets. Press the pine nuts into the pesto, cover the dish tightly with foil, then transfer to the oven and bake for 20 minutes.

3. Remove the salmon fillets from the roasting pan and stir the chopped watercress through the couscous. Season to taste with sea salt and freshly ground black pepper and some of the lemon juice, and serve with the salmon.

ROASTED MUSHROOMS WITH ARTICHOKES, BASIL & ISRAELI COUSCOUS

This dish is almost guaranteed to become a weeknight staple, but it's certainly special enough to make if you've got people over for lunch on the weekend. Israeli couscous (whole-wheat is much nicer) provides the perfect textural foil to the lemony mushrooms and artichokes. Add crumbled goat cheese or feta at the end if you wish.

Serves: 4
Prep: 10 minutes
Cook: 20 minutes

½ pound [230g] white
  mushrooms, halved
One 10-ounce [280g] jar oil-
  packed artichokes, drained
  (reserve the oil)
1 yellow onion, thinly sliced
2 cloves garlic, smashed
1⅔ cups [230g] Israeli whole-
  wheat couscous
1¾ cups [420ml] vegetable
  stock
2 tablespoons Greek yogurt
Juice of 1 lemon
Sea salt
A large handful of fresh basil
  leaves, roughly torn

1. Preheat your oven to 400°F [200°C]. Place the mushrooms, drained artichokes, 2 tablespoons of the reserved artichoke oil, the onion, garlic, and couscous in a roasting pan or large baking dish and give everything a really good stir. Add the vegetable stock, stir, cover the pan tightly with foil, then transfer it to the oven and cook for 20 minutes.

2. Remove the foil and stir in the yogurt and lemon juice. Taste and season with sea salt as needed and stir in the basil just before serving.

BULGUR WHEAT WITH ROASTED RED PEPPERS, TOMATOES, FETA & PINE NUTS

The roasted tomatoes and peppers create their own dressing for this quick bulgur wheat salad, so there's no need to add anything more, though a squeeze of lemon juice won't go amiss if you feel a citrus kick is called for. If you prefer your roasted red peppers less al dente and more charred, by all means stick them in the oven by themselves for 15 minutes before adding the cherry tomatoes and garlic.

Serves: 4
Prep: 5 minutes
Cook: 35 minutes

2 red bell peppers, seeded and
   cut into chunks
¾ pound [230g] cherry
   tomatoes
4 cloves garlic, skin on
2 tablespoons olive oil
Sea salt and freshly ground
   black pepper
⅓ cup [40g] pine nuts
1½ cups [230g] coarse
   (#3) bulgur
1⅔ cups [400ml] vegetable
   stock
3½ ounces [100g] feta cheese,
   crumbled
Fresh flat-leaf parsley leaves,
   basil leaves, or other soft herb

1. Preheat your oven to 400°F [200°C]. Place the bell peppers, tomatoes, and garlic in a roasting pan or large baking dish, drizzle with the olive oil, and sprinkle with sea salt and freshly ground black pepper. Transfer to the oven and roast for 15 minutes. Scatter over the pine nuts, then return to the oven for a further 5 minutes.

2. Add the bulgur to the roasting pan and gently stir it through the peppers and tomatoes. Add the stock and mix well so that the bulgur wheat is submerged. Cover tightly with foil, then return the pan to the oven for a further 15 minutes.

3. Remove the foil and scatter over the feta cheese and herbs. Taste and season with sea salt and black pepper as needed and serve hot.

FRESH TUNA, SCALLIONS, MANGO & CILANTRO WITH QUINOA

This quick, fresh fish recipe combines an Asian dressing with mango and quinoa for a light but flavorful dinner. Use a fairly firm mango, as it will be easier to slice.

Serves: 2
Prep: 10 minutes
Cook: 25 to 30 minutes

⅔ cup [120g] quinoa, rinsed well and drained
1½ cups [360ml] boiling water
Sea salt
Zest and juice of 1 lime
2 scallions, very thinly sliced
½ fresh red chile, finely chopped
1 tablespoon fish sauce
1 tablespoon soy sauce
1 tablespoon plus 1 teaspoon sesame oil
¼ cup [10g] finely chopped fresh cilantro
Two 4-ounce [115g] tuna steaks
1 teaspoon sesame seeds (black, if available)
1 mango, pitted, peeled, and thinly sliced

Note: A mixture of red and white quinoa adds nice color to the dish.

1. Preheat the oven to 425°F [220°C]. Place the quinoa in a roasting pan or large baking dish and cover with the boiling water. Stir in 1 teaspoon sea salt and the lime zest, cover well with foil, and transfer to the oven to cook for 20 minutes.

2. Meanwhile, to make the dressing, mix together the scallions, chile, fish sauce, soy sauce, 1 tablespoon of the sesame oil, lime juice, and cilantro. It will taste quite strong, but bear in mind it will be mixed through all the quinoa.

3. Remove the foil from the roasting pan and place the tuna steaks on top of the quinoa. Drizzle the steaks with the remaining 1 teaspoon sesame oil and sprinkle with a pinch of sea salt and the sesame seeds. Return to the oven, uncovered, for 5 minutes for tuna that's nice and pink on the inside or for 7 to 8 minutes if you prefer it cooked through.

4. Once cooked, remove the tuna and slice it. Return the slices to the roasting pan along with the sliced mango and drizzle everything with the dressing. Serve warm.

CAULIFLOWER & BROCCOLI WITH GOAT CHEESE & HAZELNUT CRUMBLE

This warming, comforting dish is a wonderful vegetarian main. You could definitely substitute Stilton or feta for the goat cheese if you prefer.

Serves: 4
Prep: 15 minutes
Cook: 45 minutes

1 medium cauliflower, cut into large florets
1 medium bunch of broccoli, cut into large florets
2 cloves garlic, smashed
3 tablespoons olive oil
Sea salt and freshly ground black pepper
½ cup [50g] skinned hazelnuts, very roughly chopped
¼ cup [55g] butter, cubed
½ cup [50g] rolled oats
½ cup [40g] panko breadcrumbs
½ cup plus 2 tablespoons [150ml] heavy cream or crème fraîche
1 cup [125g] crumbled goat cheese

1. Preheat your oven to 425°F [220°C]. Place the cauliflower and broccoli florets in a large bowl, then cover with boiling water and leave for 2 minutes. Drain well.

2. Place all the florets in a roasting pan or large baking dish and add the garlic, olive oil, and a good couple of pinches of sea salt and freshly ground black pepper. Mix well with your hands, then transfer to the oven and roast for 15 minutes.

3. Meanwhile, mix together the hazelnuts, butter, oats, panko breadcrumbs, 2 teaspoons sea salt and a good grind of black pepper and work together until the butter is evenly incorporated.

4. Once the florets have had 15 minutes in the oven, mix in the cream or crème fraîche and top with the crumbled goat cheese. Scatter over the crumble topping, then return to the oven and bake for a further 30 minutes, until golden brown and crisp.

HONEY-ROASTED CARROTS & PARSNIPS WITH QUINOA & ARUGULA

This smoky, caramelized all-in-one quinoa salad—if you are a fan of quinoa or salad—is perfect for dinner and then a lunchbox the following day.

Serves: 4 to 6
Prep: 10 minutes
Cook: 1 hour

3 carrots, peeled and cut into
  ½-inch [1.5cm] wedges
3 parsnips, peeled and cut into
  ½-inch [1.5cm] wedges
4 cloves garlic, smashed
2 large sprigs of fresh rosemary
2 bay leaves
1 tablespoon honey
2 tablespoons olive oil
2 teaspoons sea salt
Freshly ground black pepper
1⅓ cups [240g] quinoa, rinsed
  well and drained
3 cups [720ml] boiling water
1 tablespoon extra-virgin
  olive oil
Juice of ½ lemon
2 ounces [60g] arugula,
  washed

Note: Use a combination of red, white, and black quinoa for lovely color.

1. Preheat the oven to 375°F [190°C]. Put the carrots, parsnips, garlic, rosemary, bay leaves, honey, olive oil, salt, and pepper into a roasting pan, give it all a good mix with your hands, then transfer to the oven and roast for 40 minutes.

2. Add the quinoa and water, stirring and scraping the bottom of the roasting pan. Cover with foil, then return to the oven for a further 20 minutes.

3. Remove the foil, fluff up the quinoa with a fork, and leave to steam dry for 5 minutes. Drizzle over the extra-virgin olive oil, taste and season with sea salt and lemon juice as needed, then stir through the arugula. Serve hot or cold.

ROASTED LAMB WITH APRICOTS, PISTACHIOS, MINT & PEARLED BARLEY

The barley takes on all the flavor from the slow-cooked lamb and spices in this substantial dish, with the apricots bringing a balancing sweetness. It's even better warmed through the next day.

Serves: 4
Prep: 15 minutes
Cook: 1 hour

4 lamb sirloin steaks (approx. 1 pound [455g] total weight)
2 tablespoons olive oil
2 teaspoons ras el hanout
Sea salt and freshly ground black pepper
4 cloves garlic, smashed
1⅓ cups [250g] dried apricots
2 red onions, very thinly sliced
¾ cup [150g] pearled barley, rinsed and drained
1½ cups [350ml] chicken stock
Juice of ½ lemon
3 tablespoons [30g] shelled pistachios, roughly chopped
A small handful of fresh mint leaves, chopped

Note: If you prefer, slice up the cooked lamb steaks and stir them through the barley, make sure to let them rest for 10 minutes after the dish comes out of the oven.

1. Preheat the oven to 325°F [170°C]. Rub the lamb steaks with the olive oil, ras el hanout, 1 teaspoon sea salt, freshly ground black pepper, and half of the garlic and set aside.

2. In a roasting pan or large baking dish, mix together the dried apricots, red onions, the remaining garlic, the barley and the chicken stock. Place the lamb on top, cover the dish tightly with foil, then transfer to the oven and cook for 1 hour.

3. Remove the pan from the oven, taste the barley, and season as needed with sea salt, freshly ground black pepper, and lemon juice.

4. Scatter the pistachios and mint over the lamb and barley and serve hot.

ROASTED EGGPLANT WITH SQUASH, HALLOUMI, MINT & BULGUR WHEAT

Cooking the bulgur wheat in the roasting pan along with the vegetables ensures that the grains pick up all the wonderful flavors from the other ingredients. This makes a filling vegetarian main, and also works very well in lunchboxes.

Serves: 4
Prep: 15 minutes
Cook: 1 hour

1½ pounds [680g] cubed winter squash (about ½ large squash), peeled, seeded, and cut into ⅜-inch [1cm] cubes
1 large eggplant, cut into ⅜-inch [1cm] cubes
9 ounces [255g] halloumi cheese, cut into ⅜-inch [1cm] cubes
3 tablespoons olive oil
1 medium bunch of fresh mint, leaves only
A good pinch of sea salt and freshly ground black pepper
1¼ cups [200g] bulgur wheat
1⅔ cups [400ml] vegetable stock

1. Preheat your oven to 400°F [200°C]. Mix the squash, eggplant, halloumi, olive oil, half of the mint, and a good pinch each of sea salt and freshly ground black pepper in a roasting pan or large baking dish, then transfer to the oven and roast for 45 minutes.

2. Add the bulgur wheat to the roasting pan and give everything a good stir. Add the stock and mix well so that the bulgur is submerged in the stock. Cover tightly with foil, then return to the oven for a further 15 minutes.

3. Let it stand, covered, for a further 5 minutes before serving hot or cold, scattered with the remaining mint.

SPELT WITH CHORIZO, SWEET POTATO, RED ONION & SPINACH

This is a robust, substantial autumnal dinner—any leftovers will make for a really superior lunchbox. Use pearled barley if more readily available than spelt.

Serves: 4
Prep: 10 to 15 minutes
Cook: 1 hour

¾ cup [150g] spelt or pearled barley, rinsed
1½ cups [360ml] chicken stock
2 large sweet potatoes, peeled and cut into 1-inch [2.5cm] chunks
1 red onion, quartered
5 cloves garlic, skin on
½ pound [230g] Spanish chorizo, cut into ¾-inch [2cm] chunks
1 tablespoon olive oil
10½ ounces [300g] baby spinach, roughly chopped
Juice of 1 lemon
Sea salt and freshly ground black pepper

1. Preheat the oven to 350°F [180°C]. In a roasting pan or large baking dish, mix together the spelt or barley, chicken stock, sweet potato chunks, onion, and garlic. Toss the chorizo with the olive oil and scatter over the grain and veggie mixture.

2. Cover the dish tightly with foil, then transfer to the oven and cook for 1 hour.

3. Remove the foil and stir in the spinach. Season to taste with lemon juice, sea salt, and freshly ground black pepper and serve hot.

ROASTED FRUIT

THE QUICKEST OF DESSERTS—USE WHAT'S IN SEASON ALONG WITH A FEW FLAVORINGS FOR A SIMPLE, DELICIOUS FINALE TO A MEAL.

7 ROASTED FRUIT

PINEAPPLE

PLUM

RHUBARB

APRICOT

APPLE

APRICOT

PEACH

FIG

BLACKBERRY

SEE PAGE 169 FOR ROASTING TIMES

ADD FLAVORINGS

ROSEMARY

CINNAMON

LAVENDER

CARDAMOM

THYME

CHILE

GINGER

OPTIONAL

FRUIT TARTS

PASTRY

FRUIT BREAD-&-BUTTER PUDDINGS

BRIOCHE

PAIN AU CHOCOLAT   CROISSANT

COBBLERS

BISCUIT DOUGH

CRUMBLE TOPPINGS

CRUMBLE TOPPING   AMARETTI

ROASTING TIMES FOR FRUIT

FRUIT	OVEN TEMPERATURE	SUGGESTED TIME
NECTARINES (halved, pitted)	350°F [180°C]	25 TO 30 MINUTES
APRICOTS (halved, pitted)	350°F [180°C]	25 TO 30 MINUTES
PLUMS (halved, pitted)	350°F [180°C]	25 TO 30 MINUTES
PEACHES (halved, pitted)	350°F [180°C]	25 TO 30 MINUTES
FIGS (halved)	350°F [180°C]	20 MINUTES
RASPBERRIES	350°F [180°C]	20 MINUTES
BLACKBERRIES	350°F [180°C]	20 MINUTES
APPLES (whole, cored)	325°F [170°C]	40 TO 45 MINUTES
PEARS (halved, covered in wine)	325°F [170°C]	40 MINUTES
RHUBARB (covered, add some sugar)	350°F [180°C]	45 MINUTES
PINEAPPLE (cut into eighths)	350°F [180°C]	1 HOUR

Note: If your fruit is underripe it'll take longer to cook than perfectly ripe fruit, so leave it in for a bit longer and prod with a fork every five or ten minutes to check.

AMARETTI-FILLED ROASTED NECTARINES

This simple, elegant Italian dessert, suggested by Pene, this book's equally elegant art director and designer, is best made with perfectly ripe nectarines. If you have a sweet tooth, add a little sugar before stuffing them with the amaretti cookies—but they're just as lovely without.

Serves: 4
Prep: 10 minutes
Cook: 20 to 25 minutes

4 nectarines, halved and pitted
1 tablespoon dark brown sugar
  (optional)
3 ounces [80g] soft amaretti
  cookies, crumbled
¼ cup [60g] mascarpone

1. Preheat your oven to 350°F [180°C]. Place the halved nectarines cut-side up in a baking dish. Sprinkle with the brown sugar, if using, then stuff the cavities with the crumbled amaretti cookies.

2. Transfer the baking dish to the oven and roast for 25 to 30 minutes, until the nectarines are soft and the tops of the amaretti cookies are crunchy.

3. Serve immediately, with the mascarpone alongside.

HONEY-ROASTED FIGS WITH RASPBERRIES & ROSE WATER

Sometimes the simplest desserts are the best. These rose-scented figs are as good for breakfast as they are to finish dinner, and they taste unmistakably like Turkish delight.

Serves: 4
Prep: 5 minutes
Cook: 20 minutes

8 figs, halved
1¼ cups [150g] raspberries
1 teaspoon rose water
2 tablespoons honey
¼ cup [60g] Greek yogurt or crème fraîche

1. Preheat your oven to 350°F [180°C].

2. Place the figs and raspberries in a baking dish. Mix together the rose water and honey, then drizzle the mixture over the fruit. Transfer to the oven and roast for 20 minutes.

3. Serve the fruit hot, with the yogurt or crème fraîche alongside.

DATE & WALNUT CINNAMON-STUFFED ROASTED APPLES

I have something of a fear of apple corers, but if you are feeling brave (as I encourage myself to be when I want a nice autumnal dessert), I can think of few things nicer than these sticky date and walnut cinnamon-stuffed apples. Serve with ice cream or lightly sweetened mascarpone on the side.

Serves: 5
Prep: 10 minutes
Cook: 40 to 45 minutes

5 small eating apples (such as Braeburns)
2 tablespoons butter, softened
½ teaspoon ground cinnamon
2 tablespoons dark brown sugar
½ cup [80g] pitted dates, finely chopped
⅓ cup [40g] walnuts, finely chopped
1 teaspoon fresh thyme leaves, plus a few sprigs of fresh thyme
Ice cream or mascarpone, to serve

1. Preheat the oven to 325°F [170°C]. Core the apples with extreme care and place them snuggly in a baking dish.

2. Mash together the butter, cinnamon, and brown sugar, then mix in the chopped dates, walnuts, and thyme leaves.

3. Stuff the apples with the date mixture and place the thyme sprigs on top, then transfer to the oven and roast for 40 to 45 minutes, until the apples are tender.

4. Serve hot, with ice cream or mascarpone.

ROASTED APRICOTS WITH LAVENDER & ROSE WATER CRÈME FRAÎCHE

My friend Christine first introduced me to cooking with lavender, which works as beautifully here with fruit as it does in her signature lavender scones. As with all very simple recipes, the quality of the ingredients is important, so use the best, ripest apricots you can find.

Serves: 2 to 4
Prep: 10 minutes
Cook: 25 to 35 minutes

8 apricots, halved and pitted
¼ cup [50g] light or dark brown sugar
16 sprigs of fresh lavender
⅔ cup [150g] crème fraîche
½ teaspoon rose water, plus more to taste
1 tablespoon confectioners' sugar

1. Preheat your oven to 350°F [180°C].

2. Place the apricots cut-side up in a baking dish and sprinkle with the sugar. Scatter over the lavender sprigs, then transfer to the oven and roast for 25 minutes if the apricots are quite ripe or for 35 minutes if they're less yielding.

3. Meanwhile, mix together the crème fraîche, rose water, and confectioners' sugar. Taste and add a little more rose water by the drop as needed.

4. Serve the apricots hot with the rose water crème fraîche alongside.

SPICED PEARS
WITH ALMOND-CHOCOLATE
CRÈME FRAÎCHE

If you make no other dessert from this book, make this one. The chocolate in the almond crème fraîche melts on contact with the hot, yielding, syrupy pears—words fail. Try it and see.

Serves: 4
Prep: 10 minutes
Cook: 40 minutes

4 Bartlett pears, halved
1 cinnamon stick
1 star anise
8 cardamom pods, lightly
  crushed
One 375ml bottle muscat or
  your favorite sweet white wine
2 tablespoons honey
⅔ cup [75g] almond meal
1 cup [240g] crème fraîche
1½ ounces [40g] dark chocolate
  (70% cocoa solids minimum),
  finely grated
1 tablespoon confectioners'
  sugar

1. Preheat your oven to 325°F [170°C]. Place the halved pears, cinnamon, star anise, cardamom pods, and muscat in a baking dish, then cover with foil.

2. Transfer to the oven and bake for 20 minutes, then remove the foil and turn the pears over. Drizzle with the honey, then bake, uncovered, for a further 20 minutes.

3. Meanwhile, mix the almond meal, crème fraîche, grated chocolate, and confectioners' sugar together and set aside.

4. Serve the pears immediately, with the poaching wine and almond-chocolate crème fraîche alongside (see photo on page 164).

ROASTED PINEAPPLE
WITH CHILE SYRUP

Apart from the light topiary involved in preparing a whole pineapple, this is such an easy and delicious dessert. It's fancy enough to make for guests, but quick enough to make for yourself, for those days when you've been seduced into buying a whole pineapple, but haven't mustered the courage to deal with it yet. Serve it with good-quality vanilla ice cream on the side.

Serves: 4
Prep: 10 minutes
Cook: 1 hour

1 large pineapple
⅔ cup [125g] sugar
1 fresh red chile, thinly sliced
Vanilla ice cream, to serve

1. Preheat the oven to 350°F [180°C]. Leaving the leaves intact, remove the base from the pineapple, then cut the pineapple lengthwise into eight wedges. Slice off the core from each wedge.

2. Place the pineapple wedges in a roasting pan, transfer to the oven, and roast for 1 hour.

3. Meanwhile, place the sugar in a small saucepan and pour in just enough cold water to cover it. Cook over low heat, stirring constantly, until the sugar has dissolved, then stop stirring and increase the heat to medium. Let the syrup bubble for 2 to 3 minutes without stirring, then stir in the sliced chile.

4. About 15 minutes before the pineapple is ready, baste the wedges with half of the chile syrup.

5. Serve the pineapple hot with the remaining chile syrup drizzled over, and vanilla ice cream on the side.

FRUIT PLUS

ADD PASTRY OR BISCUIT DOUGH FOR AN INFINITE VARIETY OF FRUIT TARTS AND COBBLERS. OR USE CROISSANTS, ROASTED FRUIT, AND CUSTARD FOR RICH, FRUITED BREAD-&-BUTTER DESSERTS.

STICKY DATE, MOLASSES & COCONUT TART

There's something about medjool dates that recalls the sticky, toffee-like fruit that grows in the Narnia of the *The Magician's Nephew*. They're so tactile and yielding and lovely. If you can bear to cook with them instead of eating them greedily from the box, try this recipe.

Serves: 6
Prep: 10 minutes
Cook: 25 to 30 minutes

¼ cup [55g] butter
2 bay leaves
¾ pound [340g] medjool dates, torn in half and pitted
1 tablespoon molasses
¼ cup [60ml] water
One 10-by-15-inch [25-by-38cm] sheet frozen puff pastry, thawed
½ cup [30g] flaked or shredded unsweetened coconut
Vanilla ice cream, to serve

1. Preheat the oven to 400°F [200°C]. Melt the butter in a medium saucepan over low heat and add the bay leaves. Cook for 1 minute until aromatic, then add the dates, molasses, and water. Stir continuously for 2 to 3 minutes, until the dates have melted into a smooth paste. Transfer to a bowl and leave to cool for 5 minutes.

2. Place the puff pastry on a parchment paper–lined baking sheet. Spread the date mixture on the pastry, leaving a ¾-inch [2cm] border around the edges.

3. Scatter over the coconut, then transfer to the oven and bake for 25 to 30 minutes, until the pastry is golden brown. Serve hot, with vanilla ice cream.

PLUM & ROSEMARY TART

Plums and rosemary are such a lovely flavor match. Combined with brown sugar and a little cinnamon, the resulting smoky, caramelized fruit makes this tart, to my mind, one of the very best things to come out of this book. Do use dark brown sugar here, not granulated, for a molasses-y and utterly addictive depth of flavor.

Serves: 4 generously or 6 after a large meal
Prep: 10 minutes
Cook: 25 to 30 minutes

One 10-by-15-inch [25-by-38cm] sheet frozen puff pastry, thawed
8 plums, halved and pitted
⅓ cup [75g] packed dark brown sugar
Leaves of 1 sprig of fresh rosemary, finely chopped, plus 2 or 3 whole sprigs
1 teaspoon ground cinnamon
Vanilla ice cream, to serve

1. Preheat the oven to 425°F [220°C]. Place the puff pastry on a parchment paper–lined baking sheet. Top with the halved plums, cut-side up, leaving a ¾-inch [2cm] border around the edges.

2. Mix together the brown sugar, chopped rosemary, and cinnamon, then scatter this mixture over the plums. Pull the leaves off the whole rosemary sprigs and scatter them over the top. Pinch the corners of the pastry together to raise the edges.

3. Transfer to the oven and bake for 25 to 30 minutes, until the pastry is golden brown. Serve hot, with vanilla ice cream.

FIG & FRANGIPANE TART

Figs and rich almond frangipane are the perfect match—but don't despair if figs aren't in season. Follow the chart on pages 166 and 167 and create your own version using raspberries, sliced apricots, or pears, or a layer of raspberry jam and sliced almonds as a nod to a Bakewell tart.

Serves: 6
Prep: 10 minutes
Cook: 30 minutes

¼ cup plus 1 tablespoon [75g] butter, softened
⅓ cup [75g] superfine sugar
¾ cup plus 1 tablespoon [100g] almond meal
⅓ cup [50g] all-purpose flour
2 eggs
One 10-by-15-inch [25-by-38cm] sheet frozen puff pastry, thawed
5 fresh figs, quartered

1. Preheat the oven to 400°F [200°C]. If you don't have a food processor, beat the butter and sugar with a wooden spoon until light and fluffy, then stir in the almond meal and flour. If you do have a food processor, simply blitz these ingredients together. Add the eggs one at a time, beating or blitzing well after each egg, until the mixture is completely smooth.

2. Place the puff pastry on a parchment paper–lined baking sheet and spread the frangipane mixture all over it, leaving a ¾-inch [2cm] border around the edges. Pinch together the corners of the pastry to raise the edges, then top with the quartered figs.

3. Transfer to the oven and bake for 30 minutes, until the top is puffed up and evenly golden brown. (It will rise in an interesting way, but subside on cooling.) Serve warm.

ORANGE-SCENTED PEACH & BERRY COBBLER

As befits an American-inspired dish, this fruit cobbler is unashamedly generous, and the orange and almond biscuit topping is, like Mr. Bingley, extremely agreeable. Any leftovers will make an excellent breakfast.

Serves: 6
Prep: 15 minutes
Cook: 30 to 40 minutes

2¼ pounds [1kg] peaches, pitted and quartered
3½ cups [500g] blueberries or blackberries
1 teaspoon orange flower water or 1 tablespoon orange juice
1⅔ cups [200g] all-purpose flour
¼ cup plus 2 tablespoons [50g] almond meal
2 teaspoons baking powder
1½ teaspoons cream of tartar
¼ teaspoon baking soda
¼ cup [50g] superfine sugar, plus 1 tablespoon for sprinkling
Zest of 1 orange
3 tablespoons butter, cut into small cubes
½ cup [120ml] whole milk
Whipped cream, to serve

Note: If you prefer a less rustic appearance, brush the top of the cobbler dough with beaten egg before scattering over the sugar.

1. Preheat your oven to 350°F [180°C]. Mix the peaches, blueberries or blackberries, and orange flower water or orange juice in a large baking dish and set aside.

2. Stir the flour, almond meal, baking powder, cream of tartar, baking soda, ¼ cup [50g] sugar, and the orange zest together in a large mixing bowl, then add the cubed butter. Work in the butter with your hands until the mixture looks like fine sand, then make a well in the center and pour in the milk. Mix with a fork and then your hands until you have a firm, very slightly sticky dough.

3. Break off walnut-size portions of dough, pat them down into rounds, and arrange them on the peaches and berries. Sprinkle the 1 tablespoon sugar on top, then transfer to the oven and bake for 30 to 40 minutes. (If your peaches aren't perfectly ripe, bake the cobbler for a little longer.) Serve hot, with whipped cream.

RHUBARB & GINGER OAT CRUMBLE

I don't think it's possible to have too much ginger with rhubarb, and this version of the classic uses fresh ginger with the filling and ground ginger in the topping. If you're anything like me, you'll burn your tongue out of unrestrained greed as soon as the crumble comes out of the oven—but try not to—it's worth waiting five minutes for.

Serves: 6 to 8
Prep: 15 minutes
Cook: 45 minutes

1¾ pounds [800g] rhubarb,
   roughly chopped
2 inches [5cm] ginger, grated
Zest and juice of 1 orange
¾ cup [150g] granulated sugar
½ cup [50g] rolled oats
4 tablespoons butter
¼ cup plus 2 tablespoons
   [50g] all-purpose flour
¼ cup [50g] dark brown sugar
1 teaspoon ground ginger
Ice cream, to serve

1. Preheat the oven to 400°F [200°C]. Mix the rhubarb, grated ginger, orange zest and juice, and granulated sugar in a baking dish, cover with foil, then transfer to the oven and bake for 15 minutes.

2. Meanwhile, work the oats, butter, flour, brown sugar, and ground ginger together until roughly combined.

3. Remove the foil from the baking dish and give the rhubarb a good stir, then scatter over the crumble topping. Return to the oven and bake for a further 30 minutes, until golden brown and crisp on top.

4. Serve hot, with ice cream. It's also lovely, like Bridget Jones, just the way it is.

CHOCOLATE APPLE BRIOCHE PUDDING

If Marie Antoinette had written a guide to cooking, I'm fairly sure she'd say that this recipe, based on my friend Sophia's, is a wonderful way to use up leftover brioche. Suffice to say it's bread-and-butter pudding on acid—and your kitchen will smell suitably decadent once you start stirring together the melted butter, sugar, and apples, too.

Serves: 6 to 8
Prep: 10 minutes
Cook: 30 to 35 minutes

10 ounces [280g] brioche rolls
3½ ounces [100g] dark chocolate, roughly chopped
1 pound [455g] apples, peeled, cored, and cut into thin wedges
2½ tablespoons butter
½ cup [100g] sugar
1⅔ cups [400ml] half-and-half
3 egg yolks

1. Preheat the oven to 400°F [200°C]. Tear up the brioche rolls and place in a baking dish along with the chopped chocolate.

2. Pop the apples, butter, and sugar into a saucepan and cook over medium heat for 5 minutes, stirring constantly, until the apples are coated with the butter and sugar.

3. Add the half-and-half and cook for a further 1 minute, then fish out the apple pieces with a slotted spoon and put them into the dish with the brioche and chocolate.

4. Whisk the egg yolks in a large liquid measuring cup, then pour in the hot half-and-half, whisking continuously until completely incorporated. Pour the mixture into the baking dish and press down on the brioche and apples.

5. Transfer the baking dish to the oven and bake for 25 to 30 minutes, until golden brown and crisp. Serve immediately.

MANGO & COCONUT RICE PUDDING

This dish is based on the classic Thai sticky rice with mango. It has a bit of fresh ginger for a kick, and you can sweeten it to taste with light brown sugar, or with palm sugar if you have any about. It's an almost completely effortless dessert.

Serves: 4
Prep: 5 minutes
Cook: 50 minutes

¾ cup plus 2 tablespoons [180g] Thai jasmine rice
Two 14.5-ounce [400g] cans of coconut milk
2 inches [5cm] ginger, grated
2 heaping tablespoons light brown sugar or palm sugar, plus more to taste
Honey (optional)
2 ripe mangoes, peeled, pitted, and thinly sliced

1. Preheat your oven to 400°F [200°C]. Combine the rice, coconut milk, ginger, and sugar in a small baking dish and mix well. Cover with foil, then transfer to the oven and bake for 50 minutes.

2. Remove from the oven and stir well. Leave to rest, loosely covered with the foil, for 10 minutes.

3. Taste the rice and add more sugar or honey as needed, then top with the sliced mangoes and serve immediately.

CAKES &
OAT BARS

ONE BAKING DISH AND A LOT OF VARIATIONS.
FOLLOW THE RECIPES IN THIS CHAPTER FOR
NO-FUSS CAKES AND SNACKS.

8 CAKES & OAT BARS

BASICS

CAKE

SUGAR

EGGS

BUTTER

FLOUR

OAT BARS

OATS

SUGAR

BUTTER

CORN SYRUP

+

FRUIT

PINEAPPLE

RASPBERRIES

APRICOTS

ORANGE

DATES

CHERRIES

FIGS

STRAWBERRIES

APPLE

TEXTURE

PISTACHIOS

HAZELNUTS

ALMONDS

CHOCOLATE

SEEDS

FLAVORINGS

VANILLA

LEMON ZEST

CINNAMON

LAVENDER

CARDAMOM

COFFEE

ORANGE ZEST

SUPER-SIMPLE PLAIN SPONGE CAKE

This is the easiest, most foolproof cake recipe I know. In ounces, this works out as a cake with 4 ounces each of butter, sugar, and flour, to half the number of eggs, or a 4-4-4, with 2 eggs. My early counting skills were greatly assisted learning this formula from my mother. It doesn't have the same ring in grams, neither is it as easy to automatically scale up and down, but the cake—a light, fluffy, perfectly textured sponge—is identical.

Serves: 6 to 8
Prep: 15 minutes
Cook: 30 minutes

½ cup [115g] butter
½ cup plus 1 tablespoon [115g] superfine sugar
½ teaspoon vanilla extract
2 eggs
¾ cup plus 1 tablespoon [115g] all-purpose flour
1½ teaspoons baking powder
Confectioners sugar, to serve

1. Preheat the oven to 350°F [180°C]. Lightly butter an 8-inch [20cm] square baking pan and line it with parchment paper.

2. Whisk together the butter, sugar, and vanilla until light and fluffy, then whisk in the eggs, one at a time. Fold in the flour and baking powder.

3. Carefully spread the mixture into the prepared baking pan, then transfer to the oven and bake for 30 minutes, or until a skewer inserted into the cake comes out clean. Allow to cool in the pan for 5 minutes, then transfer to a wire rack to cool completely.

4. Once cool, dust with confectoners' sugar or follow one of the icing ideas on pages 208 and 209.

ICING

CHOCOLATE & PISTACHIO

¼ cup plus 2 tablespoons [50g] shelled pistachios, roughly chopped

2 ounces [55g] dark chocolate (70% cocoa solids minimum)

2 ounces [55g] milk chocolate (35% cocoa solids minimum)

⅓ cup plus 2 tablespoons [100g] crème fraîche or heavy cream

Note: This icing is fairly foolproof, but chocolate can be temperamental, so if the icing looks like it is about to break, don't panic. Add a splash of milk, let it sit for a few seconds to warm through, then whisk until smooth.

1. Toast the pistachios in a dry frying pan over medium heat for 4 to 5 minutes, shaking the pan frequently, until they start to smell nice and toasty. Remove to a plate to cool.

2. Chop the chocolates and place in a heatproof bowl set over a pan of simmering water. (Don't let the bottom of the bowl touch the water.) Stir until melted.

3. Remove the bowl from the heat and stir in the crème fraîche or heavy cream, mixing until, as Nigella Lawson would say, everything is glossily amalgamated.

4. Immediately spread the icing over the cooled cake. Scatter over the pistachios and leave the icing to set for a bit before slicing the cake.

JAM & COCONUT

½ cup [40g] flaked or shredded
  unsweetened coconut
4 to 5 heaping tablespoons
  raspberry jam

1. Toast the coconut in a dry frying pan
    over medium heat for 3 to 4 minutes,
    shaking frequently, until just golden
    around the edges. Transfer to a plate
    to cool.

2. Heat the jam in a small saucepan
    over medium heat for 3 to 4 minutes,
    stirring continuously, until melted.
    If you want to get rid of the seeds,
    push the melted jam through a sieve.
    Spread the jam on the cake, then
    scatter over the toasted coconut.
    Let the jam cool for 10 minutes or so
    before slicing the cake.

BLUEBERRY & BUTTERCREAM

3½ tablespoons butter, softened
2 cups [200g] confectioners'
  sugar
¾ cup [250g] blueberries

1. If you have a food processor, add the
    softened butter to it and blitz until
    light and fluffy. Add the sugar and
    blitz again until smooth. If mixing by
    hand, whisk the softened butter until
    light and fluffy, then beat in the sugar
    until smooth.

2. Spread the icing all over the cake (the
    closer to room temperature the icing
    is, the easier it will be to spread) and
    scatter over the blueberries before
    slicing your cake.

COCONUT, RASPBERRY & CHOCOLATE CAKE

This is one of my favorite cakes—all credit to Mrs. Bland, my cooking teacher at school from whom I learned a version of this recipe over twenty years ago that had glacé cherries instead of raspberries. Make this cake once, and I promise you'll be baking it regularly for the next twenty years, too.

Serves: 6 to 8
Prep: 15 minutes
Cook: 25 to 30 minutes

½ cup plus 1 tablespoon [115g] sugar
½ cup [115g] butter, softened
2 eggs
¼ cup [30g] all-purpose flour
¼ teaspoon baking powder
1½ cups [115g] shredded unsweetened coconut
½ cup [100g] chocolate chips
¾ cup [100g] raspberries
2 ounces [55g] white chocolate, chopped

Note: You can use any shape of baking pan as long as it has the same surface area as an 8-inch [20cm] square pan.

1. Preheat the oven to 350°F [180°C]. Butter an 8-inch [20cm] square baking pn and line it with parchment paper. Beat the sugar and butter until light and fluffy, then whisk in the eggs, one at a time. Fold in the flour, baking powder, coconut, chocolate chips, and raspberries, then smooth the batter in the prepared baking pan.

2. Transfer to the oven and bake for 25 to 30 minutes, until golden brown and a skewer inserted into a not-chocolatey bit comes out clean. Let the cake cool in the pan for 5 minutes, then turn it out onto a wire rack to cool completely.

3. Once the cake is cool, melt the white chocolate in the microwave in 10-second blasts, stirring in between until smooth. (Alternatively, melt the chocolate in a heatproof bowl set over a bowl of simmering water.)

4. Drizzle the melted chocolate over the cake (use a piping bag, if you like). Leave to set the chocolate, then cut the cake into squares and serve.

STRAWBERRY ALMOND CAKE

This is the same as the basic sponge cake, but with half of the flour replaced by ground almonds. You can experiment with ground hazelnuts or pistachios (particularly nice with chocolate icing), or use raspberries instead of strawberries. It's a very customizable template.

Serves: 6
Prep: 15 minutes
Cook: 25 to 30 minutes

½ cup [115g] butter, softened
½ cup plus 1 tablespoon [115g] superfine sugar
2 eggs
½ cup [60g] almond meal
½ cup [60g] all-purpose flour
½ teaspoon baking powder
¾ cup [100g] strawberries, hulled and sliced
2 to 3 tablespoons confectioners' sugar

1. Preheat the oven to 350°F [180°C]. Butter an 8-inch [20cm] square baking pan and line it with parchment paper.

2. Whisk together the butter and sugar until light and fluffy, then beat in the eggs one at a time. Fold in the almond meal, flour, and baking powder and transfer to the prepared baking pan.

3. Cover the top with the sliced strawberries, then transfer to the oven and bake for 25 to 30 minutes, until golden brown and a skewer inserted into the cake comes out clean.

4. Allow to cool in the pan for 5 minutes, then transfer to a wire rack to cool completely. Dust with the confectioners' sugar before serving.

STEAMED CHOCOLATE CARDAMOM PUDDINGS

With a slight variation to the basic cake recipe, these melted-in-the-middle puddings are rich and intense—perfect to finish a dinner party. And if you haven't tried chocolate and cardamom together before, you really should.

Serves: 6
Prep: 15 minutes
Cook: 25 minutes

½ cup [115g] butter, softened
½ cup [115g] dark brown sugar
2 ounces [55g] dark chocolate
  (70% cocoa solids minimum)
¼ cup plus 3 tablespoons
  [100ml] strong coffee
Seeds from 8 cardamom pods
2 eggs
½ cup plus 1 tablespoon [70g]
  all-purpose flour
¼ cup [30g] cocoa powder,
  plus 1 teaspoon to serve
A pinch of sea salt
¼ cup plus 2 tablespoons [90g]
  crème fraîche to serve

Note: You will need six ¾-cup ramekins.

1. Preheat the oven to 350°F [180°C]. Butter six ¾-cup ramekins and set them in a roasting pan or baking dish. Place the butter, sugar, chocolate, coffee, and cardamom seeds in a medium saucepan and heat for 3 to 4 minutes, stirring continuously, until smooth. Set aside to cool for 5 minutes.

2. Beat in the eggs, one at a time, then fold in the flour, the ¼ cup [30g] of cocoa, and the salt. Divide the batter among the prepared ramekins.

3. Pour boiling water into the roasting pan to come one-third of the way up the side of the ramekins. Cover the pan tightly with foil, then transfer to the oven and bake for 25 minutes.

4. Remove the ramekins from the pan and cool for 2 to 3 minutes. Use a paring knife to loosen the puddings from the sides of the ramekins. Turn the puddings out onto individual plates. Top with a dollop of the crème fraîche and a dusting of the remaining 1 teaspoon cocoa powder and serve.

STEAMED ORANGE & CHOCOLATE CHIP PUDDINGS

There are an infinite number of steamed puddings you can make from the same basic cake recipe—jam, ginger, chocolate. This, however, is my favorite, because my mother used to make it, full-size. The giveaway was a large orange appearing in the fruit bowl—further investigation revealed a bag of chocolate chips in the cupboard. The pudding was even better than the anticipation.

Serves: 6
Prep: 15 minutes
Cook: 40 minutes

2 clementines
½ cup [115g] butter, softened
½ cup plus 1 tablespoon [115g]
   superfine or granulated sugar
½ teaspoon vanilla extract
2 eggs
¾ cup plus 1 tablespoon [115g]
   all-purpose flour
1½ teaspoons baking powder
3½ ounces [100g] dark
   chocolate chips

Note: You will need six ¾-cup ramekins.

1. Preheat the oven to 350°F [180°C]. Butter six ¾-cup ramekins and set them in a roasting pan or baking dish.

2. Slice one of the clementines horizontally into six disks, rind and all, and place one slice at the bottom of each prepared mold. Zest and juice the remaining clementine.

3. Whisk the butter, sugar, vanilla, and clementine zest until light and fluffy, then add the eggs one by one and whisk until fully incorporated.

4. Fold in the flour and baking powder, then stir in 1 tablespoon of the clementine juice and the chocolate chips. Divide the batter equally among the molds.

5. Pour boiling water into the roasting pan to come one-third of the way up the sides of the molds. Cover the roasting pan tightly with foil, then carefully transfer to the oven and bake for 40 minutes.

6. Remove the molds from the pan. Gently run a paring knife around the edges of each pudding to loosen it from the mold. (Make sure to get the knife right to the bottom of the mold so that the clementine slice doesn't get left behind.) Turn the puddings out onto individual plates and serve immediately.

RETRO-FANTASTIC PINEAPPLE UPSIDE-DOWN CAKE

Is there anything better than a pineapple upside-down cake? Very little. I've insisted that my mother make this every year for my birthday for at least the last fifteen years. Artificially red maraschino cherries are, of course, mandatory.

Serves: 6 to 8
Prep: 15 minutes
Cook: 30 minutes

One 15-ounce [425g] can
   pineapple rings
A handful of maraschino
   cherries, halved
½ cup [115g] butter, softened
½ cup plus 1 tablespoon [115g]
   superfine sugar
½ teaspoon vanilla extract
2 eggs
1 cup [115g] all-purpose flour
1¼ teaspoons baking powder
1 tablespoon pineapple juice
   (from the can)

Note: You can use a rectangular baking pan as long as it has the same surface area as an 8-inch square pan. Trim the pineapple rings as needed to fit into the bottom of the pan.

1. Preheat the oven to 350°F [180°C]. Butter an 8-inch [20cm] square baking pan, line it with parchment paper, and butter the parchment. Arrange the pineapple rings and cherries on the paper as you wish and set aside.

2. Whisk together the butter, sugar, and vanilla until light and fluffy, then whisk in the eggs, one at a time. Fold in the flour and baking powder, then stir in the pineapple juice.

3. Carefully spread the batter over the pineapple rings and cherries and smooth the surface. Transfer to the oven and bake for 30 minutes, until a skewer inserted into the cake comes out clean. Invert onto a wire rack and remove the pan.

4. Carefully peel off the parchment and allow the cake to cool completely before slicing.

BASIC OAT BARS

This family favorite is a sweet treat that you can knock out in half an hour, without very much more effort than a little light stirring—it's an easy one to get children involved with. One of my earliest food memories is standing on a chair, stirring a batch of this mixture on the stove before (coughs) microwaving it in a buttered Pyrex dish.

Once you've got the basic mixture right, you can incorporate loads of different flavors, like the chocolate, raspberry, and hazelnut version on page 224, or try adding chopped apricots, dates, or almonds. The following is a template to get you started.

Serves: 6
Prep: 5 minutes
Cook: 35 to 40 minutes

½ cup [150g] golden syrup
½ cup plus 2 tablespoons
  [150g] butter
⅔ cup [135g] sugar
3 cups [300g] plain instant oats
A pinch of sea salt

Note: These oat bars are best made with instant rolled oats rather than the large, fancy, well-defined steel-cut oats. The former makes for a less sticky, more held-together oat bar.

You can use a rectangular baking pan as long as it has the same surface area as an 8-inch [20cm] square.

1. Preheat the oven to 325°F [170°C]. Butter an 8-inch [20cm] square baking pan and line it with parchment paper, leaving overhang for handles.

2. Place the syrup, butter, and sugar in a large saucepan and warm over medium heat for 2 to 3 minutes, stirring constantly, until completely melted.

3. Add the oats and salt and stir until evenly moistened. Transfer the mixture to the prepared baking pan and bake for 30 to 35 minutes, until golden brown on top. The bars will still be nice and soft to the touch but will set up as they cool.

4. While warm and still in the pan, cut the oat bars into squares. Let cool completely, then store in an airtight container.

CHOCOLATE, RASPBERRY & HAZELNUT OAT BARS

If you like your snacks to be dessert-like, this is the oat bar recipe for you. I've been reliably informed by my recipe testers Danielle and Paal that these are as good at room temperature as they are eaten within minutes of coming out of the oven.

Serves: 8
Prep: 15 minutes
Cook: 40 to 45 minutes

1½ cups [150g] golden syrup
½ cup pus 2 tablespoons [150g] butter
⅔ cup [135g] sugar
3 cups [100g] plain instant oats
A pinch of sea salt
3½ ounces [100g] dark chocolate, roughly chopped
¼ cup plus 2 tablespoons [50g] skinned hazelnuts, roughly chopped
1⅓ cups [160g] raspberries

1. Preheat the oven to 325°F [170°C]. Butter an 8-inch [20cm] square baking pan and line it with parchment paper, leaving overhang for handles.

2. Place the syrup, butter, and sugar in a large saucepan and warm over medium heat for 2 to 3 minutes, stirring constantly, until completely melted.

3. Add the oats and salt and stir until evenly moistened. Turn the mixture out into a bowl and leave it to cool down for 15 minutes, then stir in the chocolate and hazelnuts.

4. Transfer the mixture to the prepared baking pan, prod in some indentations, then squash the raspberries into them. Transfer to the oven and bake for 40 to 45 minutes, until golden brown on top.

5. Using the parchment handles, carefully lift the bars out of the pan, and place on a wire rack. Let cool completely before cutting into squares.

COCONUT, APPLE & CINNAMON BREAKFAST OAT BARS

I used to make a variation of these for student holidays, as a remedy for those evenings when you walk past the same six restaurants three times and no one can decide which to go into. Cue the all-day breakfast oat bar—staving off that combination of hunger and anger that now has its own abbreviation, but which back then just made me look like a loon. Make these to keep in your bag and avoid the same.

Serves: 8
Prep: 15 minutes
Cook: 40 to 45 minutes

Scant ¼ cup [75g] golden syrup
½ cup [100g] sugar
½ cup plus 1 tablespoon [125g] butter
1 teaspoon ground cinnamon
2 small eating apples (such as Braeburns), peeled, cored, and grated
½ cup [80g] pitted dates, roughly chopped
½ cup [75g] dried cranberries
¼ cup plus 2 tablespoons [50g] shelled pistachios
2 cups [200g] plain instant oats
1 cup [75g] shredded unsweeneted coconut

1. Preheat the oven to 325°F [170°C]. Butter an 8-inch [20cm] square baking pan and line it with parchment paper, leaving overhang for handles.

2. Place the syrup, sugar, butter, and cinnamon in a large saucepan and warm over medium heat for 2 to 3 minutes, stirring constantly, until melted, then add the grated apple and dates. Stir for 3 to 4 minutes, then add the cranberries, pistachios, oats, and coconut.

3. Transfer the mixture to the prepared baking pan, smooth it down well, then pop the pan into the oven and bake for 40 minutes, until lightly browned.

4. Using the parchment handles, carefully lift the bars out of the pan, and place on a wire rack. Let cool completely before cutting into squares.

INDEX

Many thanks are owed to Pene for the beautiful design and art direction—she propped the book and its author with extraordinary grace and good humor, to Tracey for invaluable advice and help in getting this project off the ground, to Poppy for recommending the book to Square Peg, and to Rowan for being such a wonderful editor and sounding board throughout. Many thanks are also owed to Grace for the lovely illustrations, to Annie and Sarah for hawk-eyed copyediting and proofreading, and of course to David for the stunning photographs and for being absolutely lovely to work with on the shoot.

I shamelessly demanded that my friends act as recipe testers to double and triple check cooking times and owe many thanks to Christine, Laura, Emma, Padmini, and Parvati (hi, Ma!) for trying the recipes and giving incredibly thorough and helpful feedback.

Danielle and Emma—I owe you both everything. If "This too shall pass" was the motto of the year, it passed with more grace and sanity for having you both there. (I still think the commune is the best plan.)

Ken, *il miglior fabbro*, the idea for this book came from your asking what you could cook in the oven; you have your answer, with my love and thanks.

And to my wonderful family, who have always supported me without question, the most thanks are owed. Vijay, Parvati & Padmini—you are an epic team to have. I am so lucky and grateful that you are my family and not some other randoms.

Rukmini Iyer is a food stylist and food writer, and formerly a lawyer. She loves creating new recipes and making food look beautiful for shoots, and when she's not styling, cooking, or entertaining, she can usually be found reading by the riverside, or filling her balcony with more plants than it can hold.

First published in the United States of America in 2018 by Chronicle Books LLC.
First published in the United Kingdom in 2017 by Penguin Random House UK.

Text copyright © 2018 by Rukmini Iyer.
Photographs copyright © 2018 by David Loftus.

Library of Congress Cataloging-in-Publication Data:
Names: Iyer, Rukmini, author.
Title: Dinner's in the oven / Rukmini Iyer.
Other titles: Roasting tin
Description: San Francisco : Chronicle Books, 2018. | First published in the United Kingdom in 2017 by Square Peg as: The roasting tin : deliciously simple one-dish dinners. | Includes index.
Identifiers: LCCN 2017030648 | ISBN 9781452168593 (hc : alk. paper)
Subjects: LCSH: Roasting (Cooking) | One-dish meals. | LCGFT: Cookbooks.
Classification: LCC TX690 .I94 2018 | DDC 641.7/1—dc23 LC record available at https://lccn.loc.gov/2017030648

Manufactured in China.

Designed by Pene Parker
Prop styling by Pene Parker
Food styling by Rukmini Iyer

10 9 8 7 6 5 4 3 2 1

Chronicle books and gifts are available at special quantity discounts to corporations, professional associations, literacy programs, and other organizations. For details and discount information, please contact our premiums department at corporatesales@chroniclebooks.com or at 1-800-759-0190.

Chronicle Books LLC
680 Second Street
San Francisco, California 94107
www.chroniclebooks.com